TSQ Transgender Studies Quarterly

Volume 5 ∗ Number 2 ∗ May 2018

The Surgery Issue

Edited by Eric Plemons and Chris Straayer

General Editors' Introduction

SUSAN STRYKER and PAISLEY CURRAH

Once upon a time, surgery was the sine qua non of transsexual discourse. Without surgery, a gender-variant person could be a cross-dresser, a butch, a fetishist, or a drag queen, but by definition that person was not a transsexual because they didn't cut their flesh. It's remarkable, in hindsight, to reflect on the peculiar power modern culture has granted to the surgical as a technique for the production of realness—that is, genital-altering transsexuals are considered (though not without contestation) to have *really* changed sex, while everyone else who strains against the naturalized pink/blue dichotomy is just dressing up and playing around. What is it about the surgical incision, and the removal or rearrangement of tissue, that historically has allowed it to confer a real change in social status?

In reading the early medical history of transsexuality, it's striking that *sex change* did not at first refer to the surgical transformation of genitalia in order for one typical genital morphology to come to resemble another. It referred specifically to reproductive capacity and function, and it was imagined in purely negative and subtractive terms. A person's "sex" was "changed" when they could no longer contribute to procreation: vasectomy and tubal ligation were sex changes just as much as penectomy, orchiectomy, oophorectomy, and hysterectomy, while vaginoplasty and phalloplasty (the surgical construction of vaginas and penises) were considered cosmetic plastic operations on par with getting a nose job (Stryker and Sullivan 2009).

This way of thinking about the relationship between surgery, sex, and social status is ancient—castration (orchiectomy) has been practiced for millennia on male human captives, slaves, and laborers as a way to move them closer to livestock in the hierarchies of life, and further from hereditary kingship—but totally in keeping with a modern biopolitical project that attends to the specific biological capacities of each and every body through techniques for managing and directing those capacities for state and statelike ends (Taylor 2002). Seen in the

TSQ: Transgender Studies Quarterly ✶ Volume 5, Number 2 ✶ May 2018 **161**
DOI 10.1215/23289252-4348593 © 2018 Duke University Press

light of transsexual surgery's history, modern reproductive medicine appears as a vast biopolitical apparatus for sex-changing us all, by subjecting reproduction to control and modulation by what Paul Preciado has called the "pharmaco-pornographic regime," of which surgery is just one historically significant element (2013). The condition of "operability," as Lawrence Cohen suggests, can be considered the body's threshold to modernity (2005).

There's something almost magical about the formula of citizenship and gendered personhood that transsexuals historically have been asked to perform: proclaim your desire, submit to diagnostic authority, take this pill, cut here, sign there, and voilà: you are a person of a different sex. That formula has been changing rapidly over the past quarter century, and the status of surgery within the assemblage of transformative techniques has shifted accordingly within it, in ways that make reexamining the surgical a timely undertaking for transgender studies. As guest editors Eric Plemons and Chris Straayer point out in their own introduction to this special issue, the decentering of surgery and medicine as authorizing narratives for trans- identities was causally related to the articulation of a new "transgender" discourse in the early 1990s, in the wake of Sandy Stone's massively influential "posttranssexual manifesto" (2005). If surgery had defined the transsexual, what has its status been within the transgender?

Transnationally, there is a trend toward no longer requiring genital surgery to change legal sex, and in some contexts actually to forbid this requirement in order to comply with post–World War II antieugenics laws and provisions in international treaties that forbid nonconsensual sterilization (Transgender Europe 2017). Some trans people pursue nongenital surgeries, such as facial feminization, as a way of staking their identity claims, while some people who don't consider themselves trans pursue body modification practices once closely associated with being transsexual—as when people assigned female at birth who still identify as women desire a flat chest and have a mastectomy, or inject testosterone to bulk up better at the gym and cultivate a sexy "Lauren Bacallesque" vocal huskiness. And increasingly, "changing sex" is something many people now consider to be entirely nonsurgical: an ensemble of verbal, discursive, sartorial, social, and bureaucratic performances that lend support to a self-proclaimed gender identity that no longer seeks verification through recourse to the flesh. In a technocultural milieu awash with aesthetic surgeries of all sorts, increasingly invasive biomedical interventions into reproduction, and a plethora of emerging nonsurgical practices of gender transformation, it seems increasingly impossible to make a sharp, clean incision between what is trans and what is not, when it comes to the question of surgery and sex.

In our posttranssexual, transgender, biopolitical, pharmacopornographic global order, precisely what relationship now pertains between surgery, self, genitalia, appearance, reproduction, and citizenship? The answer to that question, of course, is that there is not a single answer to that question: to interrogate the surgical in relation to transness is to open up an entire field of inquiry into the technical manipulation of the biological within a regime of power/knowledge that implacably hierarchizes life. Mixed-media artist Juliana Curi, whose sutured plant leaves are featured on the cover of this issue, evokes precisely this sense of the surgical as a craftwork that stitches life together in new ways across the caesurae not just of sex but of species and kingdoms. In doing so, her art helps mark a very large space of investigation within which fall the narrower range of topics addressed by the contributors to *TSQ*'s special issue on surgery. As Plemons and Straayer suggest, the work collected here offers a useful jumping-off point for that broader, deeper, and longer conversation, which we hope will continue taking place in the pages of this journal and elsewhere in the years ahead.

Susan Stryker is associate professor of gender and women's studies and director of the Institute for LGBT Studies at the University of Arizona and general coeditor of *TSQ: Transgender Studies Quarterly*.

Paisley Currah is professor of political science and women's and gender studies at Brooklyn College and the Graduate Center of the City University of New York and general coeditor of *TSQ: Transgender Studies Quarterly*.

References

Cohen, Lawrence. 2005. "Operability, Bioavailability, and Exception." In *Global Assemblages: Technology, Politics, and Ethics as Anthropological Problems*, edited by Aihwa Ong and Stephen J. Collier, 79–90. Oxford: Blackwell.

Preciado, Paul. 2013. *Testo Junkie: Sex, Drugs, and Biopolitics in the Pharmacopornographic Era*. New York: Feminist Press.

Stone, Sandy. 2005. "The *Empire* Strikes Back: A Posttranssexual Manifesto." In *The Transgender Studies Reader*, edited by Susan Stryker and Stephen Whittle, 221–35. New York: Routledge.

Stryker, Susan, and Nikki Sullivan. 2009. "King's Member, Queen's Body: Transsexual Surgery, Self-Demand Amputation, and the Somatechnics of Sovereign Power." In *Somatechnics: Queering the Technologisation of Bodies*, edited by Nikki Sullivan and Samantha Murray, 49–61. Farnham, UK: Ashgate.

Taylor, Gary. 2002. *Castration: An Abbreviated History of Western Manhood*. New York: Routledge.

Transgender Europe. 2017. "Legal and Social Mapping." Transrespect versus TransphobiaWorldwide (TvT) project. transrespect.org/en/research/legal-social-mapping (accessed December 27, 2017).

Introduction
Reframing the Surgical

ERIC PLEMONS and CHRIS STRAAYER

This special issue of *TSQ: Transgender Studies Quarterly* explores the vital and contested place of surgical intervention in the making of trans bodies, theories, and practices. It investigates surgery as an institutionally, culturally, politically, and personally situated practice.

Surgery is hard to talk about. This has been the case in transgender studies since the emergence of the field, often dated to the publication of Sandy Stone's essay "The *Empire* Strikes Back" in 1991 (2006). Perhaps the most influential of Stone's arguments was the call then for transsexual people—and, later, for scholars of transgender studies—to decenter, refract, complicate, or refuse the medical discourses that had for decades defined transsexuals as a group constituted by the desire for sex-altering surgical intervention. Even the handful of extant transsexual autobiographies circulating at the time, Stone argued, placed a too large and often magical focus on the kind of total transformation that surgery could have, and were, as a result, complicit with the dominant medico-surgical narrative of transsexualism as an identity and as a project that exchanged one binarily construed body for another. Stone's essay marked the beginning of thinking trans otherwise. With so many things to say and think about and with trans folks, medical discourses that focused on the fulcrum of surgery simply weren't sufficient. Instead, Stone argued, posttranssexuality could make room for new stories told by trans folks in embodied and kaleidoscopic ways. But in this multiplicity, the status of the surgical is left unsettled. Work in transgender studies has more often ignored or deflected the surgical question than engaged with it.

Stone's decentering of medico-surgical discourse has done a great deal to direct the kinds of work that have been recognized under the rubric of transgender studies, and the themes of her manifesto have animated the prevailing trends in trans politics of the last twenty-five years. Surgery, too often fetishized in

TSQ: Transgender Studies Quarterly ★ Volume 5, Number 2 ★ May 2018
DOI 10.1215/23289252-4348605 © 2018 Duke University Press

popular discourse as the act that makes the trans person real—in that surgical desire makes them *really* trans and surgical intervention materializes their *real* identity—is now most often treated in trans studies as a subject of admonition. Discussions of surgery appear in much the same way that Michel Foucault describes discussions of the masturbating child in *History of Sexuality* (1978): it is talked about mostly to remind people not to talk about it so much. But as Foucault's arguments against the "repressive hypothesis" show, we talk about what we are not supposed to talk about all the time. Policy debates about trans health care, to pick one important example, nearly always center on the contested practice (and price) of complex reconstructive surgery. The current controversy over trans people in the US military revolves around who should foot the bill for surgical operations and who will fight on the frontlines if legions of trans soldiers are languishing in postoperative recovery rooms. The considerable body of literature critiquing gatekeeping protocols for diagnosis and treatment often takes aim at processes that restrict access to surgeries.

The downplaying and decentering of surgical discourse is often intended to push thinking and conversation about trans people away from lurid and voyeuristic concerns with dissected body parts, and into deeper consideration of trans identities and lives. This can be done to lay claim to a definition of trans lives and bodies outside and in defiant rejection of medical models overdetermined by normative genders and sexualities, and to assert extraclinical and never-clinical trans ways of being. It can be a political gesture to enable coalition with other marginalized communities. But for all the good reasons to turn attention away from surgery as fascination and as fetish, refusals to talk about surgery have had unintended effects.

The practice of surgical intervention in the name of transforming sexed and gendered bodies has been happening in many parts of the world for centuries. The earliest documented case of patient and surgeon sharing a common goal of surgically reconstructing genitals to change the patient's sexed body from "male" to "female," and thus her social status from "man" to "woman," happened in Germany nearly one hundred years ago.[1] Over time, new centers of practice around the world have surged and waned in popularity as techniques are developed and practitioners' reputations grow—for good or ill. While surgeons are busy at their craft, trans social networks crackle and expand, moving information and strategic resources about how to access services, and about which procedures, doctors, and hospitals are desirable, and which should be avoided. Demand for trans-specific surgical procedures has not subsided in the thirty years since surgical discourse has been decentered in trans theory and politics; rather, it has grown.

Among the benefits of engaging surgery in this forum is that we can both collectively acknowledge the ways that past and contemporary fixations on surgery have been problematic, reductive, exclusionary, and violent, and also open urgently needed discussions about the ways that ongoing surgical practices shape the lives, bodies, and futures of many trans folks and the policies that enable and constrain them. The desire to undergo a surgical operation is often a major organizing force in the lives of prospective surgical patients, influencing decisions about where to live, what work to pursue, what school to attend, and how to manage travel, insurance, investments, savings, personal safety, and intimate relationships. Surgical outcomes profoundly change trans peoples' bodies—sometimes resulting in self-actualizing triumph and other times in crushing disappointment and lifelong chronic health problems.

We think it is important to pay attention to the practices of trans surgery, the contexts and conditions in which it happens, the professional and institutional networks in which it is carried out, the techniques employed in its name, and the understandings of sex, gender, and indeed trans itself that its practices enact. We study trans surgical practice—historically, conceptually, materially, ethnographically—not because surgery defines us as trans people, but because it is so very important to so many of our lives. We engage with surgical discourse because of the many ways that it has metonymically grounded attacks against trans people's rights to legal recognition, medical care, and even life itself. Working to break this metonymic link by merely disavowing the centrality of surgical discourse to many trans lives—even for trans-identified people who do not seek surgery—does not allow a needed engagement with these discourses, their histories, or effects.

Patient-Doctor Relations

Surgery is a physical meeting between patient and doctor and, for each, the vertex of a complex array of intentions, potentials, limitations, and concerns. The patient's outcome cannot be dislodged from social positions and interdependencies, resources and abilities, and the surgeon's skill does not exist independently of medical, ethical, legal, or economic frameworks. As a group, these essays avoid generalizations and reifications of trans people and health-care professionals and attend to a variety of individual circumstances and particulars.

Transgender medicine presents a wide spectrum of patient-doctor relations, as even a brief historical survey in the United States shows. At one end of the spectrum, patients have expressed idealizing appreciation for those who endorsed and facilitated their physical transformations (see Plemons 2017: 77–83). Christine Jorgensen chose her name in honor of her doctor, Christian Hamburg (Jorgensen 1967: 120). After becoming a patient of Dr. Harry Benjamin in 1963, Reed Erickson founded the Erickson Educational Foundation (EEF), which provided Benjamin with three annual grants to research transsexualism, drawing on his patient files and working with colleagues (Devor and Matte 2007: 60). More than simply his own clinical observations, Benjamin's files contained information and thinking provided to him by his trans patients who, like Erickson, wanted to help others like themselves.

The Erickson Educational Foundation also provided substantial funding for the Johns Hopkins Clinic, the first university-based gender identity clinic in the United States to offer sex-reassignment surgery, which opened in 1966 (60). In his many extraordinary efforts to foster the development of services for and understanding of transsexuals, Erickson considered the needs of trans people and medical professionals to be complementary (54). From 1969 through 1973, the EEF funded the first three international symposia on gender identity; they led in 1979 to the formation of the Harry Benjamin International Gender Dysphoria Association (HBIGDA) (62–63), which in 2007 became the World Professional Association for Transgender Health (WPATH). In contrast to EEF's original vision of "shared social goals between trans people and the professionals who worked with them" (54), some trans folks and their advocates have critiqued WPATH and other regulating bodies for the ways that facilitating some forms of medico-surgical intervention in the name of trans medicine has also meant restricting others. Much of this tension has centered on dynamics between (prospective) patients and the mental health-care providers whom the *Standards of Care* advise to access eligibility and prepare and refer for particular bodily alterations.

If one end of the spectrum of patient-doctor relations is collaboration, the other is conflict. The dominant tendency on the part of health-care providers, particularly psychiatrists, to pathologize the expression of trans feelings led to adversarial relationships between many doctors and patients. Agnes, a patient of Dr. Robert Stoller at the University of California, Los Angeles, Gender Identity Clinic in the late 1960s, obtained approval for sex-reassignment surgery by asserting her intersex physicality while withholding information about use of her mother's birth control pills for self-medication. Notwithstanding Agnes's competence, the eventual revelation of her dishonesty (Garfinkel [1967] 2006), alongside reports of patients' postsurgery regret from Drs. John Money and George Wolff of Johns Hopkins Clinic, reinforced an already paternalistic attitude toward trans people's subjectivities. According to the EEF newsletter, Drs. Wolff and Money concurred that a "two-year preoperative probationary period in the complete female role should take place to prevent uncertain diagnosis or inability to adjust" (EEF 1970: 2; EEF 1971: 2). Hence just as patient dispositions toward doctors have ranged from approval to antagonism so too have doctors' attitudes toward patients.

The Broader Context

Although the abbreviated history above is specific to the United States, the aspirations and conundrums it documents are not. Throughout the twentieth and early twenty-first centuries, people in many countries have sought medico-surgical interventions to alter sex and gender signifying bodily characteristics. How desires for these kinds of interventions are perceived and categorized, and how responses to them are organized, vary around the world for a number of interconnected reasons. These include locally specific conceptualizations of sex and gender and how variations from norms are understood as objects (or not) of intervention (Jarrín 2016; Winter 2009); differing political economies of health and health care; divergent philosophies of medicine; arrays of spiritual and theological traditions and their varied integration into health care and healing practices (Najmabadi 2013); technical limitations of capacity reflecting uneven distributions of material and knowledge resources; and the frictive travel of categories such as "transsexual" and "transgender" and the protocols of diagnoses and treatment through which they move (Aizura 2009), including powerful transnational documents like the *DSM* and ICD (Drescher, Cohen-Kettenis, and Winter 2012), and through nongovernmental organizations invested in "transgender" as a particular kind of figure that must be counted and protected (Dutta and Roy 2014; Thomann and Corey-Boulet 2015).

The history of trans patient-doctor relations in Argentina, for example, where surgical sex reassignment for trans folks was outlawed from 1967 until 2005 (Cabral and Viturro 2006), is different than in the Netherlands, a country whose national health service has provided trans-specific medical and surgical care for decades and has been a global hub of research on trans mental and physical health. While specific national histories vary, however, the need or desire for individuals seeking medico-surgical intervention to partner with medical professionals is common. Increasingly, though not unproblematically, trans health is becoming a transnational issue, and there is a world of alternative narratives of adversity and support, collaboration and contention.[2]

Though the texts included in this issue are wide ranging in their critiques and styles, we want to acknowledge their limited geographic and historical scope. With the exception of Joshua Franklin's ethnography of trans women confronting and making use of publicly funded surgical procedures in contemporary Brazil, all the pieces in this issue are situated in anglophone countries with a shared British colonial history: the United States, Canada, and Australia. These pieces, therefore, represent a narrow window into the practices and discourses of a mode of bodily intervention that happens in many forms throughout the world. We are unreservedly pleased, however, with the high quality of scholarship and variety of insights collected here, while nonetheless aware of the considerable breadth of perspectives, histories, subjectivities, practices, and dynamics that remain unrepresented. Our hope in this issue is to invigorate a scholarly discussion of surgical practice, while acknowledging that any such discussion will be incomplete until it is enriched and challenged by those whose voices are too often left unheard.

Thematic Concerns

What are we talking about when we designate some surgeries as "trans"? Is it a certain set of procedures that we reference? Or a particular subjective end toward which those procedures are aimed? Is it a question of legal or institutional legibility? The articles in this issue, taken together, show "trans surgery" to be a category straining against the profusion of possibilities generated by the conjunction of its constituent terms: *trans* and *surgery*. It is not surprising that it is hard to pin down just what "trans surgery" is or what might be counted as an instance of it, nor is it surprising that the stakes for doing so would be so high. What any person or institution means when they invoke *trans* as an identity, category of person, mode of politics, body project, subject of intervention, or means of thinking is constantly in flux (even orthographically, as is demonstrated by the variable use of *trans*, *trans-*, *trans**, and *transgender*). And though we can simply define *surgery* as the manual craft of altering bodies to relieve afflictions (see Cressida J. Heyes and J. R. Latham in this issue for a complication of this framing), defining its relationship to *trans* is not so simple. The diagnostic entity *transsexualism* emerged as one constituted by surgical desire (Benjamin 1954). But while clinical discourses held a monopoly over both the definition and treatment of transsexuals for decades, inscribing and reinscribing desperate surgical demand as its defining characteristic, clinicians' voices are no longer the only ones heard on the matter. If surgery is used to treat, ameliorate, or cure, what kinds of treatment is it enacting, and for what kinds of affliction? Is surgery a strategy for accessing resources such as legal standing or sex-determined labor or kinship practices, or a means through which to make a claim to them? As the articles published in this issue demonstrate, there are many ways of answering these questions, and the answers are both conditioned by and help to produce a range of ethical, institutional, and deeply personal realities.

In This Issue

In "When Building a Better Vulva, Timing Is Everything: A Personal Experience with the Evolution of MTF Genital Surgery," Sandra Mesics recalls a surgical team's "cold and dismissive" response to her pursuit in the mid-1970s for post-vaginoplasty orgasmic function. In "Busting Out: Happenstance Surgery, Clinic Effects, and the Poetics of Genderqueer Subjectivity," J. Horncastle puts forward a poetics of selfhood to counter the difficulty of asserting desire for a non-gender-normative body within clinical contexts that compromise agency. In "Surgical

Subjects and the Right to Transgender Health in Brazil," Joshua Franklin deems Brazil's legal guarantee of genital surgery to trans people to be insufficient for satisfactory life outcomes because it elides crucial social and economic dimensions of stigmatization and discrimination. In "Medical Transition without Social Transition: Expanding Options for Privately Gendered Bodies," Katherine Rachlin insists that a "real-life experience" is not only detrimental but also irrelevant to those patients who seek to alter their bodies but not change their social or legal gender. In "Trans Surgeries and Cosmetic Surgeries: The Politics of Analogy," Cressida J. Heyes and J. R. Latham oppose the tendency to cast trans people as sufferers to support an argument for psychiatric medical necessity to obtain gender surgery. Although they allow for the benefit of some gatekeeping process, they insist it should not exceptionalize trans people's relation to suffering and gender and norms or their access to surgery. How health-care professionals understand and negotiate clinical encounters, including approval for surgery, is the central matter of Riki Lane's article, "'We Are Here to Help': Who Opens the Gate for Surgeries?"

All the articles share the perspective that trans and gender-diverse patients seek access to treatment free from pathologizing scrutiny, while acknowledging that treatment providers need to assure themselves that they are not enacting harm and that they can protect themselves against charges of malpractice for competently performed surgeries in the event of patient regret. Beyond that, each article pursues a methodologically and topically distinctive focus.

Within her personal testimony, Mesics points to a grassroots network of gathering and sharing medical information in the 1970s. This was important in her situation because many surgeons still considered a transsexual woman's sexual pleasure secondary to the goal of visible morphology or, worse, clinically irrelevant. The active peer network that informed Mesics surgical encounters was also important because proactive tracking of surgical developments and studious involvement in the production and circulation of medical knowledge prefigured today's community health care.

Interviewing a variety of clinicians at the Monash Health Gender Clinic, Lane examines how clinical protocols and attitudes have changed eight years after the clinic was briefly closed, owing to two postoperative regret–related lawsuits. Lane finds that many doctors have reduced their reliance on mental health workers' diagnoses of gender dysphoria for protection against lawsuits, and they resist being characterized as gatekeepers. Indeed, some openly expressed what could be called "doctor's regret" at having denied surgery to certain patients under past guidelines. Without ignoring the experiences of trans and gender-diverse people, Lane inquires into the experience and thinking of health-care professionals, facilitating what Havi Carel and Jane Macnaughton (2012) term "second-person perspective." They remind us that an examining doctor oscillates between positions of objective observer and experiencing subject, just as patients do in their own way. Emphasizing this subjective component may make doctors more approachable to patients. Lane's article encourages doctors and patients to "coproduce" clinical encounters in ways that can rebalance the power dynamics and improve the experience for all concerned.

In a different way, Horncastle confronts questions of categories, aims, and techniques when undergoing mastectomy as part of cancer treatment. Horncastle relates their experience of a "happenstance" clinical trajectory that "devoured rather than understood" their thinking about gender and health care. Although critiquing medical care practices, they do not advocate resistance here. Rather, they ask, "Where else can the nonnormative subject turn for succor?" Their answer is poetics. Horncastle turns to poetics as a means of claiming back a body whose legibility was made precarious through attenuated and unstable relations to protocols and permissions, and the struggle to make themselves understood to clinicians caring for a cancer-stricken and genderqueer body. From a personal and medical experience not coincident but rather peripheral with trans, they redeploy theorization for restoration, to create a "landscape that in turn provides succor."

Rachlin encounters the tensions and inadequacies of guidelines tuned to an understanding of "trans surgery" as the physical component to a simultaneously social transition, and contends with what that narrow framing means for clinical relationships, patient experiences, and collective politics. Rachlin sidesteps politics in her advocacy for trans diverse subjects not often included in the "umbrella" of trans identity politics (Davidson 2007). Those who seek gender-affirming surgery but decline trans visibility as such can be both inadvertently and deliberately excluded from scholarship on trans medical care. However, their case foregrounds an important but underemphasized role that psychologists fill in the surgical process. For decades, trans-friendly psychologists, social workers, and other mental health professionals have not just assessed patient suitability for surgery but also effectively facilitated access to surgery for their patients (van Eijk 2017).

For the trans women interviewed by Franklin, whose needs and goals relevant to postoperative employment and social proficiency are not attended to by Brazil's regimented national health care, it is the mandate rather than the availability of counseling that is punitively disrespectful. Franklin describes interviewee Laura, who felt her two years of group therapy had been important, but whose steadfast optimism frustrated the clinical team. Franklin asks, "What does it mean to desire *too much*, and what does it mean when clinicians point this out?"

Heyes and Latham argue not only against a disciplinary psychiatric diagnosis but also against a political use of psychology that situates a problem within trans individuals instead of problematic systems. They parse the rhetorical strategies by which "cosmetic" and "trans" surgeries are made to be analogous or disanalogous, showing how the relationships between these modes of surgical intervention implicate historical, economic, therapeutic, and moral framings of each, and how their valence relies on the precarious figure of "suffering." In their sophisticated analysis of trans ressentiment, they caution that an investment of suffering into trans subjectivity misses the wider range of trans experiences as well as many reasons and paths toward surgery.

The essays in this issue offer more information and critical deliberation than we can summarize here. Our hope is that this special issue supports and incites further research and writing on trans and gender-nonconforming surgery and helps us to see new ways to think of it and to ask after it—whatever *it* is. We thank our contributing authors for their intellectual work. We also thank *TSQ* general editors Susan Stryker and Paisley Currah, editorial assistant Abraham Weil, and the many scholars who generously reviewed submissions, offering even those not published here attentive readings and productive criticism. We appreciate all these gifts to the scholarly project.

Eric Plemons is assistant professor in the School of Anthropology at the University of Arizona, and a faculty affiliate of the Transgender Studies Initiative there. He is the author of *The Look of a Woman: Facial Feminization Surgery and the Aims of Trans- Medicine* (2017).

Chris Straayer is associate professor at New York University and the author of *Deviant Eyes, Deviant Bodies* (1996). He serves on the editorial board of *TSQ: Transgender Studies Quarterly*. His current research project, "Trans-Physicalities," addresses transgender desires for a biological basis, neurological renditions of sexual corporeality, and trans-future medicine.

Notes

1.   The practice of transforming social status via surgical alteration of sex characteristics began long before the modern notion of "changing" sex to an opposed category. Surgeries that changed social status include circumcision; castration; penile subincision; cutting of the vulva, labia, and clitoris; vaginal obliteration; and interventions that alter internal organs' reproductive capacity. Dating the advent of surgical sex reassignment to "nearly one hundred years ago" names the first known instance of a procedure performed in which both patient and surgeon shared a common aim that the performed procedure would alter the sexed body parts—and so sex status of the requesting individual—from one binarily conceived sex category to another (Abraham 1931).

2.   For a review of international research by topic, including a discussion of the challenges of "global" research on a group whose definition is not globally shared, see Reisner et al. 2016.

References

Abraham, Felix. 1931. "Genitalumwandlung an zwei männlichen Transvestiten" ("Genital Reassignment on Two Male Transvestites"). *Zeitschrift für Sexualwissenschaft* 18: 223–26.

Aizura, Aren. 2009. "Where Health and Beauty Meet: Femininity and Racialisation in Thai Cosmetic Surgery Clinics." *Asian Studies Review* 33, no. 3: 303–17.

Benjamin, Harry. 1954. "Transsexualism and Transvestism as Psycho-Somatic and Somato-Psychic Syndromes." *American Journal of Psychotherapy* 8: 219–30.

Cabral, Mauro, and Paula Viturro. 2006. "(Trans)Sexual Citizenship in Contemporary Argentina." In *Transgender Rights*, edited by Paisley Currah, Richard M. Juang, and Shannon Minter, 262–73. Minneapolis: University of Minnesota Press.

Carel, Havi, and Jane Macnaughton. 2012. "'How Do You Feel?': Oscillating Perspectives in the Clinic." *Lancet* 379, no. 9834: 2334–35.

Davidson, Megan. 2007. "Seeking Refuge under the Umbrella: Inclusion, Exclusion, and Organizing within the Category Transgender." *Sexuality Research and Social Policy* 4, no. 4: 60–80.

Devor, Aaron, and Nicholas Matte. 2007. "Building a Better World for Transpeople: Reed Erickson and the Erickson Educational Foundation." *International Journal of Transgenderism* 10, no. 1: 47–68.

Drescher, Jack, Peggy Cohen-Kettenis, and Sam Winter. 2012. "Minding the Body: Situating Gender Identity Diagnoses in the ICD-11." *International Review of Psychiatry* 24, no. 6: 568–77.

Dutta, Aniruddha, and Raina Roy. 2014. "Decolonizing Transgender in India: Some Reflections." *TSQ* 1, no. 3: 320–37.

EEF (Erickson Educational Foundation). 1970. "An Important Message from John Money." *EEF Newsletter* 3, no. 2: 2.

———. 1971. "Symposium Spotlights." *EEF Newsletter* 4, no. 4: 2.

Foucault, Michel. 1978. *History of Sexuality*. Vol 1. New York: Pantheon Books.

Garfinkel, Harold. (1967) 2006. "Passing and the Managed Achievement of Sex Status in an 'Intersexed' Person." In *The Transgender Studies Reader*, edited by Susan Stryker and Stephen Whittle, 58–93. New York: Routledge.

Jarrín, Alvaro. 2016. "Untranslatable Subjects: Travesti Access to Public Health Care in Brazil." *TSQ* 3, nos. 3–4: 357–75.

Jorgensen, Christine. 1967. *Christine Jorgensen: A Personal Autobiography*. New York: Paul S. Ericksson.

Najmabadi, Afsaneh. 2013. *Professing Selves: Transsexuality and Same-Sex Desire in Contemporary Iran*. Durham, NC: Duke University Press.

Plemons, Eric. 2017. *The Look of a Woman: Facial Feminization Surgery and the Aims of Trans-Medicine*. Durham, NC: Duke University Press.

Reisner, Sari, Tonia Poteat, JoAnne Keatley, Mauro Cabral, Tampose Mothopeng, Emilia Dunham, Claire Holland, Ryan Max, and Stefan D. Baral. 2016. "Global Health Burden and Needs of Transgender Populations: A Review." *Lancet* 388, no. 10042: 412–36.

Stone, Sandy. 2006. "The *Empire* Strikes Back: A Posttranssexual Manifesto." In *The Transgender Studies Reader*, edited by Susan Stryker and Stephen Whittle, 221–35. New York: Routledge.

Thomann, Matther, and Robbie Corey-Boulet. 2015. "Violence, Exclusion, and Resilience among Ivoirian Travestis." *Critical African Studies* 9, no. 1: 106–23.

van Eijk, Marieke. 2017. "Insuring Care: Paperwork, Insurance Rules, and Clinical Labor at a US Transgender Clinic." *Culture, Medicine, and Psychiatry* 41, no. 4: 590–608.

Winter, Sam. 2009. "Cultural Considerations for the World Professional Association for Transgender Health's *Standards of Care*: The Asian Perspective." *International Journal of Transgenderism* 11: 19–41.

Trans Surgeries and Cosmetic Surgeries

The Politics of Analogy

CRESSIDA J. HEYES and J. R. LATHAM

Abstract This article examines the various possibilities for making an analogy or disanalogy between cosmetic and trans surgeries, focusing on the suggestion that trans surgeries are medically necessary while cosmetic surgeries are not—a position that has a great deal of rhetorical force. The authors argue that this disanalogy both fails to understand the complexity of the justifications used by recipients of these diverse surgeries and should be seen as symptomatic of various attempts in medical practice to impose particular understandings of suffering, gender identity, and gender politics on trans patients. The appeal to the intense and intrinsic suffering of the trans patient because they cannot become the normatively gendered person they always believed themselves to be, the authors argue, elides the diversity of trans experience as well as coerces trans patients into a politics of ressentiment.

Keywords analogy, cosmetic surgery, transgender medicine, gender norms

A re surgeries to "change sex" like cosmetic surgery, or even just examples of it? Or are the two sets of elective procedures significantly different ethically and/ or politically? More than a question, even, an analogy or disanalogy between the two is often invoked in a throwaway phrase or rhetorical gesture. Some trans advocates, for example, reassure that trans surgeries are nothing like cosmetic surgeries, while some social critics object that both cosmetic surgeries and trans surgeries represent capitulation to social norms and should therefore be resisted for similar reasons. In other work, we have each challenged what one might call "trans exceptionalism"—any view that trans people are uniquely positioned with regard to gender norms (Heyes 2003, 2009) or should receive medical treatment unlike that offered to nontrans patients (Latham 2013, 2017a). We have both pointed out the hypocrisies and elisions that trans exceptionalist positions involve, and the way they often work to marginalize the critical perspectives of trans people.

TSQ: Transgender Studies Quarterly ★ Volume 5, Number 2 ★ May 2018
DOI 10.1215/23289252-4348617 © 2018 Duke University Press

In this essay, we continue this work by outlining four strategies through which trans and cosmetic surgeries are compared, in order to explore some of the unarticulated or underarticulated judgments about the reasons individuals have for pursuing certain kinds of surgery, as well as what sort of institutional legitimation such reasons should or can receive. In particular, we are interested in the cases in which trans and cosmetic surgeries are articulated as dissimilar from each other. Specifically, trans surgeries are often described as medically necessary, while cosmetic surgeries are positioned as superficial and fully elective. The "medical necessity" of the former is justified as the best treatment for a mental disorder, which the *Diagnostic and Statistical Manual of Mental Disorders* (*DSM*) currently calls gender dysphoria (GD). As has been well described in trans studies, the diagnosis of GD paradoxically acts to facilitate trans medical interventions while it simultaneously constrains trans people's narratives about themselves. A central part of this constraint is the appeal, embedded in the diagnosis itself and in the medical practices that surround it, to *suffering* as constitutive of being trans. The disanalogy with cosmetic surgery typically embeds the converse claim—that cosmetic surgeries are undertaken for reasons unconnected to psychosocial distress. This latter claim is clearly false. Beyond simply pointing this out, however, we want to argue that the appeal to specific forms of suffering as constitutive of GD risks a politics of ressentiment, in which the more that suffering comes to define the trans narrative, the greater the purchase of a political psychology that disallows transformative self-descriptions and action. Our purpose here is not to dispute that trans people suffer. Rather, it is to question the effects of defending how trans medical services are made available only following a diagnosis that depends on narrating a particular kind of suffering. This is a theoretically and politically significant project in part because, as media and social attention is focused toward trans lives, we find ourselves needing to justify our presence (and existence) within an ever-more disciplined discourse (e.g., Zwi 2016). How might we make possible a politics of self-transformation (and access to medical services) that allows for being trans in more ways?

Four Comparison Strategies

The very categories "trans surgeries" (or "sex-reassignment surgeries") and "cosmetic surgeries" are internally diverse and solicit different justificatory strategies. As feminist critics of cosmetic surgery have amply demonstrated, the rationales that nontrans women invoke for particular procedures vary historically, interculturally, according to the procedure's perceived relation to normative femininity, according to the health-care system in which it is interpellated, and across individuals (Gimlin 2012; Haiken 1999; Heyes and Jones 2009). Similar caveats apply to trans surgeries: while a particular trans man might see a phalloplasty as his only hope of expressing his masculine sexuality, another might narratively reconfigure a clitoris into his penis, or welcome the sexual pleasures of penetration (Latham 2016). Genital surgeries are typically represented as the most central procedures in gender transition, with peripheral (and newer) procedures, such as facial feminization, under more vigorous contestation as "optional extras" (for reasons of technological capacity, cost, and conceptual distance from the perceived determinants of sex) (Talley 2014: 78–105). This is often not how trans people themselves perceive medical interventions, especially as genital surgeries are typically the most expensive procedures, which many are yet to be able to access. In the medical imagination, as in the popular one, the diverse procedures that move under the signs "cosmetic surgery" or "trans surgery" have different relationships to medical need or social consequence, and in a lot more cases than may be immediately apparent, patients must be careful to situate themselves appropriately to qualify for medical care, government-funded rebates, insurance coverage, or emotional support. It would be the work of another article to try to capture the actual internal complexity of these two categories, but the fact that they both serve as shorthand provides further evidence that analogizing or disanalogizing them has become largely a set of rhetorical flourishes serving political purposes.

Rhetorical comparisons between trans surgeries and cosmetic surgeries fall into four categories. First, there are those who want to suggest that trans surgeries are *like* cosmetic surgeries, and that both are medically unnecessary and undertaken for ethically suspect reasons. The nature of the ethical disapprobation is different for different commentators: some critiques of both trans and cosmetic surgeries argue that they reinforce oppressive gender stereotypes, in which people pursuing either type of surgery are chastised as troubled victims of false consciousness who engage in self-mutilation (e.g., Jeffreys 2014). For others, trans and cosmetic surgeries are alike in that they are motivated by politically naive dissatisfaction with appearance or are conformist practices undertaken for reasons of fashion, and are thus "nonessential." This view casts trans and cosmetic surgeries as frivolous and superficial, to be permitted (perhaps with concomitant moral disapproval) only as free-market transactions, not in either case as medically necessary procedures (see Vincent 2000, 2001). This analogy is also used in less overt terms to justify *denying* health-care coverage for trans surgeries and other medical interventions (see, e.g., J. Brown 2015; Draper 2015).

Second, for some commentators, cosmetic surgeries and trans surgeries can be fruitfully compared without either being judged negatively. For example, Riki Ann Wilchins imagines a dialogue between an authoritative and condescending doctor and a cowed prospective candidate for a nose job who feels like "a small-nosed woman trapped in a large-nosed body." Diagnosed with "rhino-identity disorder," the patient is refused surgery on demand and is required to "live as a small-nosed woman for three years" before qualifying (Wilchins 1997: 63;

see also Wilchins quoted in Drescher 2002: 76–81). Here Wilchins parodies the very medical framework that, for other commentators, *legitimates* trans surgeries by distinguishing them from cosmetic surgeries. Her analysis implies that the freedom of choosing a surgical intervention like a nose job ought to be available to those contemplating trans surgeries. Similarly, Dean Spade writes:

> I reject the narrative of a gender troubled childhood. My project would be to promote sex reassignment, gender alteration, temporary gender adventure, and the mutilation of gender categories, via surgery, hormones, clothing, political lobbying, civil disobedience, or any other means available. But that political commitment itself, if revealed to the gatekeepers of my surgery, disqualifies me. One therapist said to me, "You're really intellectualizing this, we need to get to the root of why you feel you should get your breasts removed. How long have you felt this way?" Does realness reside in the length of time a desire exists? Are women who seek breast enhancement required to answer these questions? (2003: 21)

Here Spade objects to the disciplining effects of a therapeutic approach that insists on a particular story about being "troubled" over a long period. He obliquely points out that there is much less disciplining for women seeking cosmetic surgery on their breasts—although the answer to his rhetorical question is not as clear a "no" as he might imagine. Paul B. Preciado extends this analogy to the use of hormones:

> I refuse the medico-political dose, its regime, its regularity, its direction. I demand virtuosity of gender: to each one, its dose; for each context, its exact requirement. Here, there is no norm, merely a diversity of viable monstrosities. I take testosterone like Walter Benjamin took hashish, Freud took cocaine, or Michaux mescaline. And that is not an autobiographical excuse but a radicalization (in the chemical sense of the term) of my theoretical writing. My gender does not belong to my family or to the state or to the pharmaceutical industry. My gender does not belong to feminism or to the lesbian community or to queer theory. Gender must be torn from the macrodiscourse and diluted with a good dose of micropolitical hedonist psychedelics. (2013: 397)

Arguably, these comments imply a normative conclusion: trans surgeries (or hormones) *ought* to be available just as cosmetic surgeries are.

Third, there is the disanalogy according to which trans surgeries are perverse, while cosmetic surgeries are acceptable forms of self-improvement. No one in the literature defends this position in these overt terms, but medicine produces and polices this boundary in precisely this way (see Latham 2017a;

Whitehead and Thomas 2013). As Virginia Goldner summarizes, "while we approve, indeed applaud, any and all efforts at excellence in masculinity or femininity that 'improve' upon the gender that is concordant with one's sex assignment at birth, we fear and despise any gestures toward confounding that gender, or crossing over to the 'other' one" (2011: 160). Take, as one example, the first penis transplant in the United States, performed in 2016 on Thomas Manning, a survivor of penis cancer. "He wants to be whole again," said surgeon Curtis Cetrulo, while the first words attributed to Manning himself by the *New York Times* are "I want to go back to being who I was" (Grady 2016). Discourses of sacrifice, restitution, and merit permeate discussions of penis transplants, with the anxious desire to reassure the public that while the procedure is "cosmetic" (in the sense that one can live a physically healthy life without a penis), it is psychologically critical. Reporting on the use of the procedure for injured veterans, the most prominent constituency with genital-urinary injuries, journalist Denise Grady writes:

> Some doctors have criticized the idea of penis transplants, saying they are not needed to save the patient's life. But Dr. Richard J. Redett, director of pediatric plastic and reconstructive surgery at Johns Hopkins, said, "If you meet these people, you see how important it is."
>
> "To be missing the penis and parts of the scrotum is devastating," Dr. Redett said. "That part of the body is so strongly associated with your sense of self and identity as a male. These guys have given everything they have." (2015)

When discussing surgical interventions to that part of the body "so strongly associated with your sense of self and identity as male," lingering in the background, of course, are genital surgeries for trans men. Soon enough the comparison comes to the fore:

> Although surgeons can create a penis from tissue taken from other parts of a patient's own body—an operation being done more and more on transgender men—erections are not possible without an implant, and the implants too often shift position, cause infection or come out, Dr. Redett said. For that reason, he said, the Johns Hopkins team thinks transplants are the best solution when the penis cannot be repaired or reconstructed. If the transplant fails, he said, it will be removed, leaving the recipient no worse off than before the surgery. (Grady 2015)

Trans and nontrans surgeries are directly in contrast here: surgeries offered to trans men are presented as insufficient and inadequate to men who are not trans.[1] The purpose of this surgery, then, is positioned as explicitly *reconstructive*:

Ultimately, the goal is to restore function, not just form or appearance, Dr. Brandacher [the scientific director of the reconstructive transplantation program at Johns Hopkins] emphasized. That is what the recipients want most. "They say, 'I want to feel whole again,'" Dr. Brandacher said. "It's very hard to imagine what it means if you don't feel whole. There are very subtle things that we take for granted that this transplant is able to give back." (Grady 2015)

Trans men writing about their own experiences have, for some time, described in agonizing detail what it is like to live as a "man without a penis" (e.g., Prosser 1998, 2005), as well as the "psychological uplift" offered through obtaining one (Martino 1977: 255; see also Cotten 2012). While trans people have argued that their experience of obtaining surgeries may also be reconstructive, and in part medical treatment for trans people rests on this assumption, it has its limits: "'Once this becomes public and there's some sense that this is successful and a good therapy, there will be all sorts of questions about whether you will do it for gender reassignment,' Dr. Kahn [a bioethicist at the same hospital] said. 'What do you say to the donor? A 23-year-old wounded in the line of duty has a very different sound than somebody who is seeking gender reassignment'" (Grady 2015). Importantly, a donor is always deceased, so the doctor here is referring to the donor's next of kin. But by obscuring this distinction, the justification for offering this surgery to nontrans men seems more obvious: a man might give up his penis to another man, and certainly, the bioethicist implies, a patriotic American man might be more likely to do so for a serviceman injured in combat. "Somebody seeking gender reassignment," then, becomes less deserving by contrast. The reason seems to be that they never had a penis in the first place and, perhaps, are thus not really men. Would a donor's family be willing to donate their deceased husband's/ brother's/son's penis to a *transgender* man? This is different, the doctor implies, and "raises all sorts of questions"; trans surgeries are not reconstructive, they are perverse.

Medical Necessity, Suffering, and the Trans/Cosmetic Disanalogy

It is the fourth analogical strategy, however, that has the longest history and the most powerful rhetorical punch for advocates of trans medical interventions: justifications for trans surgeries often rest on the notion of medical necessity through a contrast with cosmetic surgeries. At its most basic, the argument runs like this: while cosmetic surgeries are optional extras that are motivated by vanity or whim and have a relatively superficial impact on a recipient's life, gender-reassignment surgeries are necessary because of the severity of the mental disorder they effectively treat (see Holden 2016). The governing body of trans medical treatment, the World Professional Association for Transgender Health (WPATH), puts it this way: "The medical procedures attendant to gender affirming/confirming surgeries are not 'cosmetic' or 'elective' or 'for the mere convenience of the patient.' These reconstructive procedures are not optional in any meaningful sense, but are understood to be medically necessary for the treatment of the diagnosed condition. In some cases, such surgery is the *only* effective treatment for the condition, and for some people genital surgery is essential and life-saving" (Knudson et al. 2016: 3). Trans surgeries are here understood as remedial for GD. As we know, to be a "sufferer" of GD—and hence to qualify for trans surgeries (and other interventions) in contexts in which qualifications are determined in reference to *DSM* and WPATH diagnostics—typically requires that one construe these interventions as a restitutive project, in which the subject is brought home to an originary, hitherto invisible identity (Prosser 1998). In this model, gender is understood as essential, stable, predetermined, and beyond the control or choice of the individual. For example, in speaking about her discrimination case against the insurance company, Aetna, Ashlyn Trider says: "This is a medical condition. I was born with it. It's medically necessary surgery. My doctor has strongly urged this procedure get done. It's pretty straightforward" (quoted in Draper 2015). It also typically requires that trans people express a desire for a conventionally sexed body that aligns with a more-or-less conventional gender—within the medical discourse of restitution, ongoing ambiguity is anathema (e.g., see Latham 2018; Sullivan 2008). Finally, GD is distinguished by the severity of its symptoms: David Valentine reports that, among his informants, trans surgeries are "the only possible solution to life-long suffering and a struggle with the sexed body and its social and personal meanings; it is no more a choice than any other medical procedure that might save a life" (Valentine 2012: 192).

A diagnosis of GD is accompanied by a narrative about gender identity that individual patients must adopt to qualify for medical treatment, to greater or lesser degrees, depending on their physicians and health-care system. For some trans people, the narrative description of GD in the *DSM* is a remarkable fit with their lived experience; for those who do not fully identify with it, however, it leads to constraints on individual self-description that have been criticized within trans studies for a long time (see, e.g., Latham 2017a; Stone 1991; Stryker 1997). To obtain a GD diagnosis, someone seeking trans services must describe themselves as already belonging to an alternative sex-gender category. Thus the surgeries or other services a trans person receives are not positioned in themselves as transgendering (or sex changing) but *gender confirming*. That is, instead of saying, "I want to become a man," a trans man is expected to explain himself by saying (in the GD vernacular articulated by the *DSM*), "I was always a man inside and I need my body to match." This distinction is important, as it acts in disallowing particularly gender-nonconforming interventions such as, most obviously, genital surgeries without matching hormone use, but a whole host of other combinations of interventions as well. That medicine acts this way purposefully is a point emphasized in the eunuch movement: men who desire castration in order to live as "eunuchs," "a third sex," or "something other than male" are routinely denied treatment on the basis they do not present an appropriate gender identity to receive services (see Vale et al. 2010). The American Psychiatric Association stresses this distinction in the *DSM*: "Some males seek castration and/or penectomy *for aesthetic reasons* or to remove psychological effects of androgens *without changing male identity*; in these cases, the criteria for gender dysphoria are not met [and thus surgical interventions should be withheld]" (APA 2013: 458; our emphasis).

The disanalogy with cosmetic surgery contributes to this reasoning by providing a false counterpoint centered on the nature and degree of the suffering involved. Consider, for example, the following reasoning, contained in part of Commissioner Mary Ross Hendriks's opinion in a case brought through the provincial human rights tribunal against the Canadian province of Ontario when it delisted trans surgeries from health-care coverage: "The Complainants, through their pleadings, in their own testimony, and in the testimony of their witnesses, have recounted to the Tribunal the needless suffering and loss of dignity that the de-listing of sex reassignment surgery has caused to both themselves and to the very small number of others with profound GID [gender identity disorder, the precursor to GD] who require sex reassignment surgery in order to live their lives in equanimity as opposed to tragedy" (2005: §43). In Hendriks's judgment (as in others), the rhetorical contrast with cosmetic surgery stands in for a deeper understanding of trans surgeries as necessitated by psychological suffering that can only be remediated by surgery. This implicates the argument in a number of corollaries: that a key marker of GD is suffering of a specific and identifiable kind; that those who want cosmetic surgery do *not* suffer (or, at least, not as much as trans people, and not enough to cross some threshold for insurance coverage); and that suffering (and the negative mental health sequelae it engenders) is central to making appeals to medical services. These are all controversial claims that would be difficult to investigate empirically and even harder to conclusively justify. Although there is plenty of psychological research on both trans and (to a lesser extent) cosmetic surgery, suffering is notoriously conceptually difficult to quantify or even to describe phenomenologically.

Thus, rather than debating the precise extent or the nature of the suffering that trans people experience, we want to make an argument about the risky political effects of crystallizing in law or public policy a subjectivity premised on psychosocial suffering. To do this, we draw on feminist critiques of ressentiment, which is, in its original Nietzschean formulation, the internalization of a slave morality. Ressentiment is not simply resentment (although clearly the two words are related). Instead, as Wendy Brown reformulates it, ressentiment describes the paradoxical attachment of the socially marginal to the very wounded identities they claim to want to surpass (1995). For many political movements, characterizing and gaining legitimation for a shared experience of powerlessness and suffering has been a central political project. The danger of ressentiment, however, is that such characterizations will be taken up in the psychic life of individuals, as well as circulated in various ways through the polity, such that transformative, active self-understandings and political projects meet with an often tacit or even unconscious resistance. In Brown's words, ressentiment "fixes the identities of the injured and the injuring as social positions, and codifies as well the meanings of their actions against all possibilities of indeterminacy, ambiguity, and struggle for resignification or repositioning" (1995: 27). This is the first main danger that feminist critics have stressed; the second is that political ressentiment may also rely on and reinforce the very relations of power that it claims to oppose (Stringer 2000). For example, Mariana Valverde comments that "some reflections on the perils of mentoring that can be found circulating (verbally) among younger feminists, suggest that ethical problems can develop when women who have gone through hardship but have then 'risen' persist in seeing themselves exclusively as victims in need of support" (2004: 86).

Glimmers of this critique appear in the texts we have already referenced. Wilchins, for example, remarks: "To get surgery, you have to mount what I call an Insanity Defense. *I can't help myself, it's something deep inside me, I can't control it. It's degrading.* . . . In a civilized society, wanting what you want and getting help should not require you to accept a psychiatric diagnosis, produce a dog-and-pony show of your distress, and provide an identity to justify its realness" (1997: 191–92). The risk of this rhetoric is that this show of distress will come to signify the essence of the trans individual—and ultimately, for those who take a biomedical perspective to its logical conclusion, the meaning of their bodies. As Spade puts it, the presumption that to be trans is to be "desperate," and that only suffering individuals would request trans surgeries, is "a fundamental part of the medical approach to transsexualism." In recounting his own experience, he tells us that "the therapists I've seen have wanted to hear that I hate my breasts, that the desire for surgery comes from desperation." He asks, "What would it mean to suggest that such desire for surgery is a joyful affirmation of gender self-determination—that a[n] SRS candidate would not wish to get comfortable in a stable gender category, but instead be delighted to be transforming—to choose it over residing safely in 'man' or 'woman'?" (Spade 2003: 21).

To describe everyone defending access to trans surgeries by referencing suffering as trapped in a politics of ressentiment would be obviously simplistic, as well as insulting. There is a risk, however: the more suffering comes to define the trans narrative, the greater the purchase of a political psychology that individualizes gender and disallows critique of the systems that contribute to trans people's suffering in the first place. Sandy Stone anticipated this problem almost thirty years ago when she wrote, "What is lost is the ability to authentically represent the complexities and ambiguities of lived experience" (1991: 295). These complexities include positive experiences of sexuality, comfort with ambiguous anatomy, acceptance of a discontinuously gendered life, or (most pointedly perhaps) critique of the psychiatric systems that discipline trans patients.

There is also a converse critique: the suggestion that cosmetic surgery is undertaken by people (mostly women) who "just" want to look good but who could take or leave a particular intervention glosses over and trivializes the diverse lived experiences of its recipients. Cosmetic surgery *is* often justified on the grounds of extreme psychological suffering—even (perhaps especially) when the bodily "flaws" that recipients hope to correct are within "normal" range (e.g., Blum 2003; Davis 2009; Gimlin 2006; Heyes 2007; Jones 2008). Kathy Davis (1995) famously made this argument in her early work with Dutch women who were, not coincidentally, attempting to secure state funding for cosmetic procedures. This suffering is not only descriptive of a particular subjectivity but also similarly produced by a particular scene of address: some cosmetic surgery recipients are interpellated (and interpellate themselves) into contexts in which their emotional pain or desire for normality acts as a counterpoint to the charges of superficiality and vanity that seeking out cosmetic surgery can provoke. As Eric Plemons argues, "The benefits of enhanced self-esteem or the personal peace that comes from an integrated and socially legible body are used to justify many surgical procedures" (2014: 46; see also Benatar 2006). Arguments from suffering are often, and often successfully, used by nontrans people to enable insurance/public coverage for procedures that are considered borderline cosmetic (e.g., Australian Government 2014; Essig 2010). Although beyond the scope of this article, the scene of address clearly includes specific health-care institutions: privatized medicine delivered through insurance companies places different demands on citizens than public systems, and those that have precedent for covering procedures traditionally thought of as cosmetic differ again from those that have never permitted them (see here Edmonds 2007, 2013 on Brazil; Gimlin 2012 for a cross-cultural analysis of the United Kingdom and United States).

To give a detailed example, Diane Naugler (2009) argues that breast reduction surgery sits uncomfortably on the line between the reconstructive and the cosmetic. The Canadian patients she interviewed used a number of tactics to urge that the intervention be understood as the former, thus justifying their right to a provincially funded surgery. Much like many trans people, they researched the reasons they would have to provide to physicians to be convincing, and they emphasized (or downright fabricated) the physical pain of very large breasts as well as the psychosocial suffering they experienced. Physical pain is, at least in this context, safer ground: it is an unverifiable yet epistemically significant experience. The psychosocial aspect of their self-descriptions, however, was more problematic: Naugler's interviewees needed to frame their suffering through the lens of a normative femininity. They wanted smaller breasts because they hated the (hetero)sexual attention large breasts brought, but they could not want breasts smaller than a C-cup since that would risk removing *all* such attention, which many (hetero-male) surgeons assume is enjoyable for women (or even a condition of adequate femininity). Butch candidates could not risk honestly characterizing the forms of sexual attention they objected to (or wanted); nor could they invoke their embodied identity as grounds for wanting small (or no) breasts (see Butler 2004: 85–87; Latham 2017b: 188). The appeal to suffering here, then, is intertwined with a normative identity: only a particular *kind* of suffering will do, and the actor's capacity to give it meaning is limited (as well as encouraged) by the medical gatekeeper. This example shows how, just as with trans surgical appeals, suffering is incorporated in ways that risk ressentiment and limit agency: some kinds of pain were irrelevant, others needed to be framed or emphasized in strategic ways, and the absence of pain was a contraindication for surgery.

Thus appeals to suffering do not distinguish trans from cosmetic patients, and in both cases suffering needs to be understood within intersubjective political contexts that are not only enabling but also constraining for individuals. The risk of ressentiment is present in both cases but exaggerated for trans patients because of the scripted personal narratives that the diagnosis of GD typically requires. The disanalogy between trans and cosmetic surgeries likewise glosses over the ways that cosmetic surgeries are incorporated by health-care systems, while coverage for the treatment of GD is disallowed. While advocates for trans surgeries might attempt to differentiate them through recourse to medical necessity (as in the WPATH example above), in practice "medical necessity" is consistently used by nontrans patients to access both public and private health coverage for cosmetic procedures. That is, as we saw in the penis transplant example, psychosocial suffering justifies medical treatment. Similarly, breast removal surgeries for gynecomastia ("male breast development") are available in many Western health-care systems to those designated male (but not female), on the grounds that to be a man with "female-appearing" breasts is traumatic (e.g., see Barros and Sampaio 2012). Trans men may access breast removal surgeries only upon proving themselves to be men (through obtaining a GD diagnosis); female persons who identify as women can never access breast removal surgeries unless they have cancer or some other independent health reason for needing a mastectomy. As Naugler's work shows, while all women are required to want breasts of some size, breast reduction is permitted only if it fits with a normative gender presentation. Thus access to surgery is managed not through the degree of suffering as a marker of medical necessity but, rather, through conformity to a normative understanding of sex-gender of which GD is a neat part.

Conclusion: Self-Determination and Individualized Care

Medically necessary and *medically indicated* are nebulous terms that are often used for obtaining cosmetic surgeries in which the justification of "improved psychosocial functioning of the patient" is routine and acceptable. The question, then, is why trans people cannot access the same interventions without undergoing considerable psychiatric scrutiny aimed at matching them to a detailed narrative diagnosis. It is an established point in trans studies but, it seems, one that persistently disappears: the GD diagnosis dictates a subjectivity by describing a past, present, and future of required self-understanding that is organized just as much around the gender norms upheld by those who wrote it as by observation of trans patients. This diagnosis is disciplinary, not merely descriptive.

GD is resistant to this critique, and trans treatment protocols more broadly are resistant to antipsychiatric critique, for many historical, conceptual, and political reasons. A central justification of GD from trans critics is that it provides access to health care (or insurance) for trans people. Whether this is true is, in part, a research question that could be answered only by empirical study of the interface between trans patients and diverse health-care systems, and while we reference some of this work, we have not drawn any novel empirical conclusions here. Rather, by unpacking the assumptions buried in a disanalogy between trans and cosmetic surgeries, we hope to have shown that the assumption that GD must be accompanied by defined expressions of suffering originating exclusively in the individual carries political risks, while the characterization of cosmetic surgery as not medically necessary because psychologically trivial is so clearly false that it can only serve as an empty rhetorical counterpoint. Instead, both trans and cosmetic surgeries are justified or withheld within health-care systems using the language of medical necessity. As we have shown, going back behind this language reveals it to be invested in gender conformity in both sorts of cases.

Still, we are clear that access to medical services (including surgery) is important and valuable for many trans people, and it should be provided as we provide care for people with appendicitis or depression. The ultimate question is, what sort of gatekeeping is apt? We do not support completely unfettered on-demand access to any plastic surgery, but we are not psychologists and cannot elaborate what sort of counseling practice is most appropriate here. We are simply noting that whatever gatekeeping is done should not participate in hypocritical trans exceptionalism, which it currently does. As Timothy Cavanaugh and colleagues argue, "The SOC [Standard of Care]'s continued reliance on mental health professionals to determine eligibility and readiness for treatment perpetuates a message that neither the patient nor the prescribing clinician is capable of a nuanced discussion of gender variance and its management" (2016: 1150). Individual trans patients should be able to describe their past, present, and future; embodied experience and aspirations; felt sense of self; and so on, in diverse terms without being disqualified from surgery. This novel practice would also dispel the risk of ressentiment by uncoupling suffering of prescribed kinds from a singular trans subjectivity. The question "What is medically necessary for whom?," then, is one that should be decided by clinicians with their patients. Indeed, WPATH itself claims, "It is important to understand that every patient will not have a medical need for identical procedures. Clinically appropriate treatments must be determined on an individualized and contextual basis, in consultation with the patient's medical providers" (Knudson et al. 2016: 30). Ensuring just and equitable treatment must not require all trans patients to undergo identical regimes of interventions, and defending the diagnosis is not the only way to ensure access to trans interventions. As Judith Butler argues:

> Examples of the kinds of justifications that ideally would make sense and should have a claim on insurance companies include: this transition will allow someone to realize certain human possibilities that will help this life to flourish, or this will allow someone to emerge from fear and shame and paralysis into a situation of enhanced self-esteem and the ability to form close ties with others, or that this transition will help alleviate a source of enormous suffering, or give reality to a fundamental human desire to assume a bodily form that expresses a fundamental sense of selfhood. (2004: 92)

These more diverse and political aspirations apply across the board to those surgeries we have been calling "trans" and "cosmetic."

Cressida J. Heyes is professor of political science at the University of Alberta. She is the author of *Self-Transformations: Foucault, Ethics, and Normalized Bodies* (2007) and the coeditor with Meredith Jones of *Cosmetic Surgery: A Feminist Primer* (2009). Her work can be found on cressidaheyes.com.

J. R. Latham is honorary fellow in cultural studies at the University of Melbourne. His work has been published in *Aesthetic Plastic Surgery, Australasian Journal on Ageing, Feminist Theory, Sexualities,* and *Studies in Gender and Sexuality*. Visit jrlatham.com.

Note

1.   That this distinction is sexual is unsurprising, as trans people are constituted medically through sexual inadequacy (see Latham 2016).

References

APA (American Psychiatric Association). 2013. *Diagnostic and Statistical Manual of Mental Disorders*. 5th ed. Arlington, VA: American Psychiatric Association.

Australian Government. 2014. *MBS Reviews: Vulvoplasty Report*. Department of Health. www .health.gov.au/internet/main/publishing.nsf/content/vulvoplasty.

Barros, Alfred C. S. D. de, and Marcelo de Castro Moura Sampaio. 2012. "Gynecomastia: Physiopathology, Evaluation, and Treatment." *São Paulo Medical Journal* 130, no. 3: 187–97.

Benatar, David, ed. 2006. *Cutting to the Core: Exploring the Ethics of Contested Surgeries*. Lanham, MD: Rowman and Littlefield.

Blum, Virginia. 2003. *Flesh Wounds: The Culture of Cosmetic Surgery*. Berkeley: University of California Press.

Brown, Jennifer. 2015. "Health Transition: Transgender People Seek Coverage of Procedures Insurers Call Cosmetic." *Denver Post*, December 17. extras.denverpost.com/transgender /health.html.

Brown, Wendy. 1995. *States of Injury: Power and Freedom in Late Modernity*. Princeton, NJ: Princeton University Press.

Butler, Judith. 2004. *Undoing Gender*. New York: Routledge.

Cavanaugh, Timothy, Ruben Hopwood, and Cei Lambert. 2016. "Informed Consent in the Medical Care of Transgender and Gender-Nonconforming Patients." *AMA Journal of Ethics* 18, no. 11: 1147–55.

Cotten, Trystan T., ed. 2012. *Hung Jury: Testimonies of Genital Surgery by Transsexual Men*. Oakland, CA: Transgress.

Davis, Kathy. 1995. *Reshaping the Female Body: The Dilemma of Cosmetic Surgery*. New York: Routledge.

———. 2009. "Revisiting Feminist Debates on Cosmetic Surgery: Some Reflections on Suffering, Agency, and Embodied Difference." In *Cosmetic Surgery: A Feminist Primer*, edited by Cressida J. Heyes and Meredith Jones, 35–48. Farnham, UK: Ashgate.

Draper, Electa. 2015. "Transgender Woman Challenges Aetna Coverage Denial." *Denver Post*, July 29. www.denverpost.com/2015/07/29/transgender-woman-challenges-aetna-coverage -denial/.

Drescher, Jack. 2002. "An Interview with GenderPAC's Riki Wilchins." *Journal of Gay and Lesbian Psychotherapy* 6, no. 2: 67–85.

Edmonds, Alexander. 2007. "'The Poor Have a Right to Be Beautiful': Cosmetic Surgery in Neoliberal Brazil." *Journal of the Royal Anthropological Institute* 13, no. 2: 363–81.

———. 2013. "The Biological Subject of Aesthetic Medicine." *Feminist Theory* 14, no. 1: 65–82.

Essig, Laurie. 2010. *American Plastic: Boob Jobs, Credit Cards, and Our Quest for Perfection*. Boston: Beacon.

Gimlin, Debra. 2006. "The Absent Body Project: Cosmetic Surgery as a Response to Bodily Disappearance." *Sociology* 40, no. 4: 699–716.

———. 2012. *Cosmetic Surgery Narratives: A Cross-Cultural Analysis of Women's Accounts*. Basingstoke, UK: Palgrave Macmillan.

Goldner, Virginia. 2011. "Trans: Gender in Free Fall." *Psychoanalytic Dialogues* 21, no. 2: 159–71.

Grady, Denise. 2015. "Penis Transplants Being Planned to Help Wounded Troops." *New York Times*, December 6. www.nytimes.com/2015/12/07/health/penis-transplants-being-planned-to -heal-troops-hidden-wounds.html.

———. 2016. "Cancer Survivor Receives First Penis Transplant in the United States." *New York Times*, May 17. www.nytimes.com/2016/05/17/health/thomas-manning-first-penis -transplant-in-us.html.

Haiken, Elizabeth. 1999. *Venus Envy: A History of Cosmetic Surgery*. Baltimore: Johns Hopkins University Press.

Hendriks, Mary Ross. 2005. "Interim Decision of the Human Rights Tribunal of Ontario." November 9. cupe.ca/updir/Hogan_Decision.pdf. Last accessed February 26 2017.

Heyes, Cressida J. 2003. "Feminist Solidarity after Queer Theory: The Case of Transgender." *Signs* 28, no. 4: 1093–120.

———. 2007. "Normalisation and the Psychic Life of Cosmetic Surgery." *Australian Feminist Studies* 22, no. 52: 55–71.

———. 2009. "Changing Race, Changing Sex: The Ethics of Self-Transformation." In *You've Changed: Sex Reassignment and Personal Identity*, edited by Laurie J. Shrage, 135–54. New York: Oxford University Press.

Heyes, Cressida J., and Meredith Jones, eds. 2009. *Cosmetic Surgery: A Feminist Primer*. Farnham, UK: Ashgate.

Holden, Madeleine. 2016. "Three Surgeries Every Two Years: NZ's Shameful Fifty-Year Waitlist for Gender Reassignment Surgery." *Spinoff*, December 15. thespinoff.co.nz/society/15-12 -2016/three-surgeries-every-two-years-nzs-shameful-50-year-waitlist-for-gender-reassign ment-surgery/.

Jeffreys, Sheila. 2014. *Gender Hurts: A Feminist Analysis of the Politics of Transgenderism*. Abingdon, UK: Routledge.

Jones, Meredith. 2008. *Skintight: An Anatomy of Cosmetic Surgery*. Oxford: Berg.

Knudson, Gail, et al. 2016. "Position Statement on Medical Necessity of Treatment, Sex Reassignment, and Insurance Coverage in the U.S.A." World Professional Association for Transgender Health (WPATH), December 21. www.wpath.org/site_page.cfm?pk_ association_webpage_menu=1352&pk_association_webpage=3947.

Latham, J. R. 2013. "Ethical Issues in Considering Transsexual Surgeries as Aesthetic Plastic Surgery." *Aesthetic Plastic Surgery* 37, no. 3: 648–49.

———. 2016. "Trans Men's Sexual Narrative-Practices: Introducing STS to Trans and Sexuality Studies." *Sexualities* 19, no. 3: 347–68.

———. 2017a. "Making and Treating Trans Problems: The Ontological Politics of Clinical Practices." *Studies in Gender and Sexuality* 18, no. 1: 40–61.

———. 2017b. "(Re)Making Sex: A Praxiography of the Gender Clinic." *Feminist Theory* 18, no. 2: 177–204.

———. 2018. "Axiomatic: Constituting 'Transexuality' and Trans Sexualities in Medicine." *Sexualities*. Published ahead of print, January 30. journals.sagepub.com/doi/abs/10.1177 /1363460717740258.

Martino, Mario, with harriett. 1977. *Emergence: A Transsexual Autobiography*. New York: Crown.

Naugler, Diane. 2009. "Crossing the Cosmetic/Reconstructive Divide: The Instructive Situation of Breast Reduction Surgery." In *Cosmetic Surgery: A Feminist Primer*, edited by Cressida J. Heyes and Meredith Jones, 225–38. Farnham, UK: Ashgate.

Plemons, Eric D. 2014. "It Is as It Does: Genital Form and Function in Sex Reassignment Surgery." *Journal of Medical Humanities* 35, no. 1: 37–55.

Preciado, Paul B. 2013. *Testo Junkie: Sex, Drugs, and Biopolitics in the Pharmacopornographic Era.* New York: Feminist Press.

Prosser, Jay. 1998. *Second Skins: The Body Narratives of Transsexuality.* New York: Columbia University Press.

———. 2005. "My Second Skin." In *Light in the Dark Room: Photography and Loss*, 163–82. Minneapolis: University of Minnesota Press.

Spade, Dean. 2003. "Resisting Medicine, Re/modeling Gender." *Berkeley Women's Law Journal* 18, no. 1: 15–37.

Stone, Sandy. 1991. "The *Empire* Strikes Back: A Posttranssexual Manifesto." In *Body Guards: The Cultural Politics of Gender Ambiguity*, edited by Julia Epstein and Kristina Straub, 280–304. New York: Routledge.

Stringer, Rebecca. 2000. "'A Nietzschean Breed': Feminism, Victimology, *Ressentiment*." In *Why Nietzsche Still? Reflections on Drama, Culture, and Politics*, edited by Alan D. Schrift, 247–73. Berkeley: University of California Press.

Stryker, Susan. 1997. "Over and Out in Academe: Transgender Studies Come of Age." In *Transgender Care: Recommended Guidelines, Practical Information, and Personal Accounts*, edited by Gianna E. Israel and Donald Tarver, 214–44. Philadelphia: Temple University Press.

Sullivan, Nikki. 2008. "The Role of Medicine in the (Trans)Formation of 'Wrong' Bodies." *Body and Society* 14, no. 1: 105–16.

Talley, Heather Laine. 2014. *Saving Face: Disfigurement and the Politics of Appearance.* New York: New York University Press.

Vale, Kayla, et al. 2010. "The Development of Standards of Care for Individuals with a Male-to-Eunuch Gender Identity Disorder." *International Journal of Transgenderism* 12, no. 1: 40–51.

Valentine, David. 2012. "Sue E. Generous: Toward a Theory of Non-transsexuality." *Feminist Studies* 38, no. 1: 185–211.

Valverde, Mariana. 2004. "Experience and Truth-Telling in a Post-humanist World: A Foucauldian Contribution to Feminist Ethical Reflections." In *Feminism and the Final Foucault*, edited by Dianna Taylor and Karen Vintges, 67–90. Urbana: University of Illinois Press.

Vincent, Norah. 2000. "Cunning Linguists: Sex and Gender." *Advocate*, June 20.

———. 2001. "San Francisco Gives in to Theorists: Welcome to the Transsexual Age." *Village Voice*, May 21. www.villagevoice.com/news/welcome-to-the-transsexual-age-6415642.

Whitehead, Jaye Cee, and Jennifer Thomas. 2013. "Sexuality and the Ethics of Body Modification: Theorizing the Situated Relationships among Gender, Sexuality, and the Body." *Sexualities* 16, nos. 3–4: 383–400.

Wilchins, Riki Ann. 1997. *Read My Lips: Sexual Subversion and the End of Gender.* Ithaca, NY: Firebrand.

Zwi, Adam. 2016. "Transgender Children, the Law, and a Boy Born in the Skin of a Girl." *Guardian*, January 19. www.theguardian.com/commentisfree/2016/jan/19/transgender-children-the-law-and-a-boy-born-in-the-skin-of-a-girl.

Surgical Subjects and the Right to Transgender Health in Brazil

JOSHUA FRANKLIN

Abstract In 2007, a Brazilian federal appeals court ruled that gender affirming care was guaranteed on the basis of the constitutional right to health. This is part of a broader process of the "judi-cialization" of the right to health in Brazil. In this essay, the author draws on fourteen months of ethnographic fieldwork conducted at a public gender clinic in southern Brazil to consider the experiences of transgender people who accessed surgery through the expanded public services that followed the litigation. The article argues that access to surgery does not, by itself, ameliorate the intersecting forms of vulnerability and exclusion experienced by the people followed by the author. Yet despite the limitations of a focus on surgery, expanded access to care does create possibilities for trans people to engage in diverse forms of self-transformation. The paradigm of access to gender affirming care through right-to-health litigation circumscribes the possibilities for social trans-formation within a set of biomedical technologies that come to stand for more radical change. Attending to the diverse forms of care and self-governance that trans people themselves labor to enact offers a more productive register for thinking about the socially transformative potential of the judicialization of health in Brazil.
Keywords Brazil, transgender health, ethnography, right to health

I n 2007, a Brazilian federal appeals court ruled that gender affirming care was guaranteed as part of the constitutional right to health (Associated Press 2007; Ventura 2011). This decision, which came out of an *ação civil pública* (public class-action lawsuit) initiated by transgender patients within the public health-care system, is part of a broader pattern of seeking access to care through the courts, termed the "judicialization of health." As work within transgender studies has shown, the exclusive linking of legal recognition with specific kinds of medical authorization or intervention excludes many transgender people and even diverts attention from the health priorities of nonnormatively gendered people (Spade 2011; Valentine 2007). In particular, Brazilians who identify with the cultur-ally specific category of *travesti* have been unable to access care because they are illegible within the anglophone discourse of medicalized gender identity that

TSQ: Transgender Studies Quarterly ★ Volume 5, Number 2 ★ May 2018   **190**
DOI 10.1215/23289252-4348629   © 2018 Duke University Press

posits genital surgery as essential (Jarrín 2016; Teixeira 2011), a consequence of the subordination of Brazilian categories to hegemonic science (Silva and Viera 2014). Yet even if initially grounded in a biomedical model, access to gender affirming care might be taken up in different ways in a more holistic paradigm of health (Arán and Murta 2009).

In this essay, I attend to the experiences of transgender people who accessed surgery through the expanded public services that followed right-to-health litigation. What is the potential for social transformation through such a collaborative effort between transgender people, health professionals, and legal advocates to claim access to biomedical technology? I argue that access to surgery does not, by itself, ameliorate the intersecting forms of vulnerability and exclusion experienced by the people whom I followed. Yet despite the limitations of a focus on surgery, expanded access to care does create possibilities for trans people to engage in diverse forms of self-transformation.

This work draws on fourteen months of fieldwork conducted at a public gender clinic in Porto Alegre, Brazil.[1] I spent time observing in the hospital as well as outside the clinical arena. I followed patients to their homes, workplaces, and churches and spent time with their partners and families. In addition, I interviewed health professionals, lawyers, representatives of nongovernmental organizations, and scholars. I focus in detail on the stories of two transgender women, which are condensed from a series of interviews in clinical settings as well as in their homes. However, I do not claim that they are representative, nor do I mean to draw from them a coherent or totalizing narrative of Brazilian gender or transgender subjectivity. Rather, I hope to complicate the ways in which surgery is linked to subjection and belonging by addressing the complex consequences of rights-based access to biomedical technologies of gender in Brazil.

Clinical discourses produce ways of classifying people that do not capture the complexity of people's lives. As other scholars have shown, the figure of the "official transsexual" is generated in Brazil through an opposition to the categories of "travesti" and "gay" (Bento 2006: 23; Jarrín 2016). This mode of classifying does not begin to encompass the diversity of trans identity, much less the other forms of social difference with which gender is entangled. However, I am not arguing that clinicians are forcing trans people into pathologizing categories. The clinicians whom I observed were compassionate and sensitive to the social and economic challenges faced by their patients, and their work is limited by the same kinds of structural factors that impact their transgender patients (Metzl and Hansen 2014). Rather, I see the limitations of clinical discourses as a necessary starting point for understanding the experiences of transgender people and caregivers alike. This is true not only for those who are excluded from care but also for those who are able to access it.

The paradigm of access to gender affirming care through right-to-health litigation circumscribes the possibilities for social transformation within a set of biomedical technologies that come to stand for more radical change. At the same time, the stories of my transgender interlocutors point to the critical importance of ordinary and subjective modes of transformation in understanding their lives. The cases of Vitória and Laura that I discuss below illustrate the ways that clinical interventions fail to address the quotidian needs of many transgender people, but more importantly, they point toward the diversity of forms of care and self-governance that trans people themselves labor to enact. This in turn offers a more productive approach for thinking about the socially transformative potential of the judicialization of health in Brazil.

Theorist Lauren Berlant, in a conversation with Jay Prosser, warns about the risk of representing transgender people as "the inflated subjects of suffering who are only really living in relation to the transformative event or gesture" (2011: 186). The fantasy of the autonomous subject of transformation is central to the biopolitical regulation of trans people. Indeed, anthropologists, among others, have argued broadly for attention to the ordinary events that do not cohere into narratives of transformation. As Kathleen Stewart puts it, abstractions like neoliberalism and biomedicalization "do not in themselves begin to describe the situation we find ourselves in" (2007: 1).

The promise of surgical interventions might be a kind of "cruel optimism" in Berlant's words (2011). An exclusive focus on surgery, that is, might impede exactly the kinds of transformation that it promises by obscuring the more quotidian practices and forms of care that are necessary. But people can temporarily identify with a desire for transformation as part of an amalgam of strategies of the self. For this reason, I want to add to Berlant and Prosser's call for attention to the "ordinary forms of care, inattention, passivity, and aggression that don't organize the world at the heroic scale" (2011: 186). Transformation is also part of the fabric of everyday life, and it requires neither a radical politics nor a dramatized event to organize it. This refers not to a singular transformative event but, rather, to a series of acts of social recognition and orientations toward the future enacted by trans people as well as their families, legal advocates, and caregivers. This may occur within and at times be limited by neoliberal institutions—but those regimes do not exhaust its creative energy.

In what follows, I present the case of Vitória, whose story shows the possibilities that surgery enables as well as the way that medical interventions fail to address the most exigent needs of vulnerable people. I then turn to daily clinical practice to show how a complex set of desires are folded into the promise of surgery in the Brazilian context in which I worked, in part through the negation of travesti identities. I then discuss the case of Laura, whose quest to sustain a feeling of futurity in the wake of surgery shows the potentials that access to care enables but does not fulfill. I conclude by discussing, in the context of the judicialization of health in Brazil, how these cases might suggest a different register for assessing the transformative possibilities of right-to-health activism.

"Why Is This Not My Reality?"

Vitória sat across from me in the crowded café; it was the first time since her surgery that she had returned to the hospital. Her voice filled with frustration and optimism, she said:

> I am going to be free, independent. I am going to have my own money, and from there I will conquer a new life for myself, with people who don't know me. And it will be a new life for me. I want, I dream . . . I will take all the available public employment exams. I will try to do this to be able to get a guaranteed job. I want to do more things for myself. I want to get breast implants, I want to buy new clothing, I want to buy shoes; I want to become beautiful, you know? To become perfect. And unfortunately, my salary is not enough for this. So, I want to be employed and to have rights. I want to have money; I want to live. In my mind, I am very modern—a very evolved person. If I am in this situation that I am in now, it is only because I do not have another option. I have met transsexuals who are very evolved—very feminine, who have had plastic surgery for their face, who have done everything. And rich, with good clothing, with everything. I am envious of this. Why is it that this is not my reality?

I had met Vitória a month earlier, when I visited her in the hospital only days after she had undergone a gender affirming surgery. Vitória was a patient at a gender identity program operating in a public hospital in southern Brazil, one of the few to provide transition-related health care for free to poor patients through SUS (Sistema Único de Saúde), the Brazilian public health-care system.

"Since I was a child," she explained several weeks after her surgery in her home, "I have always felt myself to be a woman. And I suffered a lot in school. I felt different from the other boys." Around the time of eighth grade, she learned that she could go to the local health post to obtain hormones. But she told me that she wanted to pursue surgery: "I wanted to be a real woman." When she was twenty years old, she was referred to the gender identity program in Porto Alegre. Vitória recalled, "My heart exploded with happiness. I felt like another person." Access to surgery represented a possible future opening for Vitória.

Almost two years passed when I did not speak to Vitória, but a little more than a year and a half after her surgery, I visited her at her home. Vitória began to relate the events of the past two years: "So much has happened that when I tell you, you will be shocked."

After her surgery, Vitória became depressed. She worked at several secretarial and custodial jobs but was constantly harassed, and she never stayed in one place for long. It took almost a year for her to change her name and sex on her official documents. "I had realized my dream of becoming a woman," she told me. "Only, I wasn't able to be a beautiful woman . . . and that left me sad." Vitória didn't earn enough to afford the clothes that she wanted, so she began to do sex work at night while working her other jobs during the day. "It's a sad life, humiliated like that in the street," she said.

Vitória began a relationship with a client. He was a retired chief of police, three decades older than her, who said that he wanted to save her from her life of prostitution, and she moved into his apartment a month later. She told me that he paid for her clothing, cosmetics, and laser hair removal. At the time, she was working as an assistant at a preschool. But after a few months, she could no longer bear their arrangement. "He was very jealous. . . . It was hell to live with him; I could only bear to do it because I needed to." She was accepted for a position in public employment doing custodial work at a school. Her boyfriend moved her to a new town and continued to pay her rent.

Vitória was ambivalent about her ex-boyfriend, explaining, "He's helping me because he is religious. He likes to help people, so he is helping me. But we are not living together. He gave me a lot; he gave me clothes; he gave me everything that I needed. And now I am living the life that I always wanted." She registered this relationship as a difficult situation, not an abusive one, even though she was unequivocal about the power dynamics at play: "He was a father to me. My real father did nothing for me. *Nothing*. But him, no, he helped me with everything. Everything that I needed." Later, she said, "He wanted very much for me to fall in love with him, but I couldn't do it. He made me cry and he fought with me." It was this man who allowed her to live the life she had always wanted. Vitória told me that she could not return to sex work, no matter how much she could earn.

Gender affirming surgery for Vitória, perhaps like for many other transwomen in Brazil, meant achieving social recognition and personal actualization at the cost of gendered vulnerability to violence. Economic dependence made Vitória subject to the violent operation of male power and the emotional and psychological wounds it inflicted. Her story left me uncomfortable, especially with the entanglement of sexuality, beneficence, and fatherhood in the portrait Vitória had painted of her ex-boyfriend. I was unsettled by the intricate web of unfulfilled desires and needs, never quite spoken aloud but constellated by failed relationships and projects of transformation. Vitória, able to undergo genital surgery through SUS but not breast augmentation or facial hair removal (which were deemed cosmetic), was socioeconomically excluded from the promise of care supposedly made by the constitutional right to health.

Vitória had plans for her life now that she had a stable job. "Next year," she told me, "I want to get breast implants. . . . And then I want to apply to adopt a child." She explained that her public employment was "liberation." She fell silent as she searched for the words to express her happiness and relief. But it was clear that her experience did not conform to the medicalized narrative that posits genital surgery as radically transformative; transcendent moments were made possible by obtaining independence tied to stable employment, and by glimpsing the possibility of altering her life trajectory. Vitória's story reveals the complex dynamics of class and gender that raise the question of what it means for poor transgender Brazilians to claim the right to transition-related health care.[2]

Vitória speaks of becoming a "real" and "beautiful" woman, pointing to desires beyond her struggle to find stable employment. Beauty is an arena of unique social potency. Anthropologist Alexander Edmonds has mapped the meanings and practices of beauty and the politics of access to cosmetic plastic surgery through the public health system in Rio de Janeiro, arguing that "for some workers and consumers on the margins of the market economy, physical allure can be an asset that actually seems to disrupt the class hierarchies that pervade many other aspects of their lives" (2010: 250). This is not to deny the reality of economic power but to see the body as a distinct site that is articulated with capitalist values in complicated ways. For Edmonds, "beauty culture becomes an arena of self-governance" that must be apprehended on its own terms (104). At the same time, the norms of beauty to which Vitória aspires are themselves produced by a racialized and classed social field. As Jarrín argues in his ethnographic work on plastic surgery in Brazil, beauty itself may be understood as a biopolitical domain. Unlike Edmonds, Jarrín understands plastic surgery as a "neoliberal extension of eugenic concerns that date back to the early twentieth century" (2015: 537). Although beauty might not be equivalent to class, becoming beautiful is not a means for Vitória to escape the precarity of her situation.

But whatever the limits of its power to transcend the operation of socioeconomic class, beauty has an affective valence. Embodiment involves multiple desires inextricably joined as they are inscribed on the indeterminate body (Salamon 2010), and so I read Vitória's struggle to become a beautiful woman as, in part, an attempt to find a name for the vulnerability she experiences, even if her capacity to alter her condition is limited. In this sense, Vitória's story shows how biomedicalized notions of transformation and inclusion miss the mark, pointing to ordinary needs that access to surgery does not address.

Surgery and Identity

What patients expect from surgery is shaped by the everyday activities of the gender identity program, which serve to secure their identifications within a frame of biomedical knowledge. As the director of the multidisciplinary team, a surgeon, commented in an interview, "We separate the psychology group from the surgery group, because I do not like to have anything to do with the diagnosis. They tell me, 'this is the list of the patients you have to operate on,' and I do the operation. We divide it like this, it is a kind of ethical procedure." This leads to the institutional separation of surgical activities from psychological ones, in which the role of mental health clinicians is to provide the surgeon with patients who have "the right diagnosis." What constitutes the right diagnosis is a combination of established criteria from standards such as the *DSM* (the American Psychiatric Association's *Diagnostic and Statistical Manual of Mental Disorders*) and Brazilian health regulations. The director stressed conservative treatment decisions: "If we have a doubt, we just don't operate. We try not to harm the patients, because the harm is definitive." In this context, gender identity—and the problematic "right diagnosis"—is the basis for access to biomedical technology and social inclusion.[3]

Patients undergo a two-year period of group therapy every two weeks before being eligible for surgery. This two-year period was required by federal health regulations, although the format of group therapy was specific to this gender identity program. These therapy sessions are disruptive for many; for example, Vitória had to leave home before 5:00 a.m. to arrive for her 8:00 a.m. group therapy by bus; she did not return until the late afternoon. The requirement of such an investment of time to access surgery is one way in which the program assigns importance to the procedure and defines its relationship to the process of transformation. As Laura, who I introduce below, told me in an interview shortly before her surgery, "What is a transsexual? To be a transsexual is the fact that even though having to wait two years can be boring or inconvenient, she won't desist—she will insist, continue, and will complete those two years. Because it is a life goal."

Laura's concern to locate herself in a socially defined field of terminology relating to identity categories centered on gender and sexuality, something that represented a great deal of time in group therapy sessions I observed, reflects the extent to which patients were forced to contend with the opposition between the terms *transsexual* and *travesti*. *Travesti* is a socially recognized category in Brazil that designates individuals who are assigned male at birth and may modify their bodies through hormones and silicone injections, among other practices, use female names and pronouns, and yet do not identify as women or as transgender (Kulick 1998). As Alvaro Jarrín shows, the legitimacy of the category "transsexual" is produced through a denial of travesti identity (2016). Thus an emphasis on the body— particularly the genitals—in patients' narratives is a bid for moral and social legitimacy in its appeal to medical authority and its disavowal of a travesti identity.

Patients experience a set of multiple desires: social mobility, legal security, a sense that their identities are socially legitimate, and access to a consumer market. The discourse of gender affirmation makes it possible to articulate these as a coherent narrative of surgical transformation. Yet it is a precarious coherence, painstakingly produced in clinical interactions. During one session, a participant put forward the theory that she was a transsexual because she felt that she was almost a woman, "but for this one detail." However, she said this with some irony because she was participating in a two-year period of group psychotherapy to correct this "detail"—this detail was clearly of great importance to her. This exchange was iterated many times during my fieldwork.

Another illustrative session was spent in a tensely confrontational exchange between the psychologist and a patient, Júlia. The psychologist was trying to explain that it was possible that there would be some less-than-perfect results from the surgery, even serious complications: "You have to be conscious of the fact that you won't be one hundred percent." Júlia exclaimed, "Stop!" "What if," the psychologist asked, "you don't have pleasure afterwards?" Júlia responded, "I don't think about that, because I will!" The psychologist insisted, "If you aren't afraid, you are a little disconnected." Júlia seemed frustrated as the time for the session ran out.

However, Isabella seemed to embody the positive attitude that Júlia was reluctant to admit: she told the group that people think that the surgery "will change everything, everything will be different. But it isn't like that." She explained to the rest of the group that facing prejudice and discrimination would continue to be difficult. The surgery helps, Isabella said, but it does not change things by itself. Another patient spoke up, rejecting Isabella's focus on prejudice, and said that the most important thing was how she felt about herself and her body. The psychologist asked the entire group why they wanted the surgery, and they gave nervous, hesitating answers: "To make myself adequate," "Because I was born a woman," "Because it was always my dream." As the psychologist explained the importance of having realistic expectations from the surgery, Isabella supplied the word *fugir*—to escape—hinting at the complex desires folded into one embodied transformation.

These diverse responses show that patients are not naively optimistic or merely playing along with what they think clinicians expect. These encounters reveal the work that must be done to sustain the potential of surgery to represent social transformation. This occurs through identification with the category *transexual* and disavowal of the category *travesti*, in both explicit conversations about language and silences around topics such as sex work, as group participants were reluctant to speak about sex work, frustrating their therapists. The need to distance oneself from markers of travesti identity further ensures that practical and economic concerns will be marginalized or ignored, beyond a simple focus on genital surgery. In doing so, patients invested a great deal in the potential of surgery. Laura, whose story I discuss below, struggled to maintain this sense of futurity in the days after her surgery.

"That's the First Thing—To Believe"

Laura was frustrated and felt she could not move forward until she had genital surgery. "I had already lived as a woman for a long time before I entered the gender identity program, which shows that [the genital surgery] is a small detail," Laura told me in our first interview. She was using hormones, but she told me, as we sat in a cafe, that genital surgery was "extremely important."

After her surgery, Laura said, she would be able to change her legal sex marker, finish school, and become certified as a nurse technician. Most importantly, she told me, she would be able to find a husband; since the end of her first, eleven-year relationship, each of her relationships ended when her partner discovered that she was transgender. Laura, in her late thirties, often told me how frustrated she was that she was single.

Laura remarked to me, "The day that I die I want to put an epitaph on my grave: 'Here lies Laura, who fought her whole life against nature. Finally, nature won.'" Laura laughed and explained, "We fight against our hair, we fight against our Adam's apples, we fight against our noses, and we fight against our genitals. We fight whether or not other people know. So, we fight our whole lives against nature until the day it conquers us." Laura saw her life as a struggle, striving for bodily actualization as well as social acceptance.

When I asked Laura about her experience in group therapy, she told me that little had changed, and that "the only thing that nobody, obviously, likes is having to wait two years. Because everybody wants to have the surgery as quickly as possible. But I think that these two years, in many cases, are important." Laura explained, "I think that many people enter thinking that they know everything. . . . As time passes in the group, they see the differences of opinion and the doctors clarify things. I think that sometimes people begin to perceive that they are not transsexuals, or that they have to change a certain way of thinking about life." Laura never seemed to doubt her identity, nor did she describe her experience in therapy in terms of changing her perspective on life. She was skeptical about the possibility that some transgender people might not want to undergo genital surgery as soon as possible.

Laura had high expectations for her surgery: "My expectations are the best possible. Because, for me, it will completely change my life." Laura's surgical objectives were also social—to find a husband, to change her name. At this point, Laura had already been a patient for over a year. The team was nervous because they felt that Laura hoped to gain too much from surgery, and that they thought that she had a good chance of being disappointed with the results. What does it mean to desire *too much*, and what does it mean when clinicians point this out?

Laura met with the clinical team for a final interview, in which she would confirm her desire for surgery. The social worker asked her if she had any fears about the surgery. "None," Laura replied, "because I think that the group always serves to address our doubts. . . . So, we know that it is a surgical procedure, that it can result in pain for one person, and not for another, and that there may or may not be complications. So, we know that it will be different for everybody. But I am extremely confident in believing that everything will be completely correct."

The team pressed Laura, and the surgeon explained: "The result depends on many factors, including the genitalia that the person has, the skin, et cetera. It depends on the scar formation, and its healing. Every person is different. So, we cannot know how it will be in the end." The clinicians rightly see the need to caution Laura about the risks of surgery, and Laura struggles to find a balance between too much desire (unrealistic expectations) and too little (ambivalence about the surgery or about the genitals she currently has).

"We know that there are many people who are . . . completed, and everything transpired perfectly. So, I think that I, too, will be one of these people. I believe it, you know? Because that's the first thing—to believe," Laura said, uttering this last phrase with a slight laugh and perhaps a sense of irony; she seemed eager to move on and to avoid addressing the social worker's doubts about her expectations for the surgery. She continued, "With any kind of surgery, we know that there could be a complication or some issue. But I always believe that it isn't anything that can't be fixed or made better." The interview ended shortly after, leaving the clinical team frustrated by their skepticism about Laura's comprehension of the risks of the genital surgery. But despite their discomfort, the team decided that Laura met the criteria for undergoing surgery: she underwent a vaginoplasty and facial feminization surgery.

I visited Laura in the hospital several times during her recuperation; the day after her surgery, she was in intense pain, but that subsided quickly, and she was released six days afterward. I visited Laura at home the day after she returned there to recover, a week after the day of her surgery. Laura is poor; at the time, she had been working intermittently taking care of an elderly woman, and the house where she lived alone was a dimly lit concrete box adorned only with a small table and a makeshift bed. Her mother lived on the next street, and she was recovering there, since it was difficult for her mother to walk back and forth between the houses. Her mother's anxiety about Laura's surgery had abated, she told me, now that the most difficult part was past. Laura, however, was impatient. She said that after the first day, she felt very little pain, but she was uncomfortable and anxious for her recovery to be complete. She lamented the fact that she was still single: "I am totally alone. Me and God."

As I continued to visit Laura at home, it became clear that she negotiated her conflicts of identity outside the clinic, and a new picture of her desire emerged. Laura's relationship with biomedical knowledge and practice was complicated.

It was necessary, in her perspective, insofar as it enabled her to access medical transition. Furthermore, the power of medical authority enabled her to use her medical transition as leverage to legitimate her identity in her social world. However, emotional and practical support came from her family and religious community. At this point in her life, Laura received a great deal of support from her Seventh Day Adventist church group, which would pray weekly for Laura's successful surgery or rapid recovery. Laura tried, successfully as far as I knew, not to reveal the nature of her surgery to the church group, telling them instead that she was scheduled for an appendectomy.

I returned to Laura's home a year later. The space was still uncomfortably bare, but she had a few more pieces of furniture and had begun tiling a corner of the main room. Laura described her struggle to find work, taking course after course at a local vocational training center but never finding a job. Marcelo, her boyfriend, worked as a nighttime security guard, which he liked because it gave him time to study English. Laura told me that she hoped that if Marcelo could learn English, he would be able to find lucrative work in the tourism industry. Laura's plans to become certified as a nurse technician and to return to Europe, where she had lived decades earlier, had been abandoned, at least temporarily. Laura seemed intent to talk about Marcelo, emphasizing his role as breadwinner, although she spoke English much better than he did. Yet despite her relationship with Marcelo, life for Laura remained in a future tense, displaced onto a different job or place. In her struggle to sustain this futurity, Laura shows how her own transformation is shaped indirectly by the figure of the travesti, as she contends with these unfulfilled desires that escape the register of the surgically focused *transexual* identity.

When I returned a few weeks later and spoke to Laura alone, she confided that she was distressed about her relationship with Marcelo. Things became difficult when, during one of their first dates, she was outed in a chance encounter with Marcelo's brother-in-law. Laura took Marcelo to the shore and told him about her gender identity. "Then when I had told him everything, he said, 'Look, this doesn't make the littlest difference. You are good just as you are.'" But, she added anxiously, "I don't know if this is just a fantasy of mine, but I think that my relationship with him has never been quite the same."

Marcelo's mother cut ties with him, and he fought with his family. Laura surprisingly thought of the law in this moment: "I said that what I was going to do was enter a lawsuit against them. They will say that I am not a woman, I will say that I am a woman, I will prove legally that I am a woman, because it was the law of Brazil that gave me my documents, which state: female." I was struck by her recourse to the state when she said, "The only right I had to defend myself was to say, I am going to court, and we can fight in court." She told me that Marcelo's mother relented when she began to talk about a lawsuit, but that in the process, her community and church had all learned about the conflict. "It was a horrible thing," she told me. "It's something you just don't do, destroy the life of a person like that."

Laura had left the church group that had supported her and had been such a major part of her life in the past. A new pastor came, and he did not accept her the way that her old pastor had. From a biomedical perspective, Laura had completed the process of transition in terms of gender, but she was still in a state of suspension, waiting for a moment of transformation in terms of work and relationships to bring her the kind of happiness she wanted. I asked her how she felt about her medical transition. She answered, "I would say, 70 percent. Why not 100 percent? I think that maybe . . . although my mother doesn't think so, I think I still need some cosmetic surgery. To become a little more beautiful." I thought of Vitória, and of Laura's words before her surgery: "I always believe that there is nothing that cannot be fixed, repaired, or made better."

Judicialization and Transgender Rights

Cross-cultural work on gender variance tends to minimize political economy by assigning difference to a monolithic and immutable "culture" and ignoring the complex historical, technical, and socioeconomic production of gendered identity (Towle and Morgan 2006). Yet recent critical work within transgender studies points to the analytic importance of class difference and focusing an economic lens on issues that have been constructed exclusively as questions of "gender identity" (Irving 2008; Valentine 2007). This suggests that some rights-based strategies may fail to address the urgent needs of the most marginalized transgender people, as legal scholar Dean Spade argues, because in a neoliberal context, such advocacy is more likely to justify the very institutions that exclude nonnormatively gendered people (2011). Yet this critique may take for granted the normative force of the law, instead of interrogating it as a lived practice, as Isaac West contends (2014).

Brazil is a unique case not only because of culturally specific categories such as *travesti* but also because of the possibilities created by the right to health, guaranteed in Brazil by the constitution of 1988. Starting with HIV/AIDS activists in the 1990s, patients have successfully won the right to access health care in court, especially in the form of pharmaceuticals. The effects of this judicial activism are highly contested. Some critics argue that this "judicialization" of the right to health has been co-opted by a pharmaceutical industry eager to reshape that right as a right to consume medical technologies—especially pharmaceuticals (da Silva and Terrazas 2011; Ferraz 2011). Yet others see this phenomenon in a more positive light. As anthropologist João Biehl argues, the judicialization of the right to health in Brazil creates a space where individuals make demands on the state and achieve recognition even if on an individual basis. Drawing on a database of right-to-health lawsuits in the state of Rio Grande do Sul, Biehl and colleagues found that judicialization "largely serves the disadvantaged who turn to the courts to secure a wide range of medicines, more than half of which are on government formularies and should be available in government health centers" (Biehl, Socal, and Amon 2016). "The judicialization of health," Biehl writes, "has, indeed, become a para-infrastructure in which various public and private health actors and sectors come into contact, face off, and enact limited 'one by one' missions" (2013: 431). Not radically upending market rationality, these juridical subjects are nevertheless able to maneuver within this political field.

The federal court decision about access to gender affirming care supports this way of understanding the judicialization of health. In his 2007 ruling, Judge Roger Rios held not only that access was justified by the right to health, but also that failing to provide gender affirming care constituted gender-based discrimination prohibited by the constitution. In his view, the right of transgender people to access transition-related health care is not just a right to health in the face of pathological suffering. In an interview in Rio de Janeiro, legal and public health scholar Miriam Ventura explained that this legal creativity came from a group of legal scholars during the era of HIV/AIDS activism who believed that justice could not be reduced to the law: "All rights have an ethical foundation. Therefore, the law does not restrict rights. The law cannot restrict rights; the law must make itself adequate to rights." Judge Rios was hopeful about the social and ethical potential of this innovative vision of the law; when I asked him what was the impact of his decision to order SUS to pay for gender affirming care, he told me, "It is in the sense of breaking with the gender binary." As the stories of Laura and Vitória suggest, the possibilities enabled by such a lawsuit are not simply the value of access to surgery but also the more complex and varied subjective and social work that follows this access, even when transgender people as well as health and legal professionals struggle to render it visible in official discourse.

Conclusion: Surgical Subjects

While biomedical technology may stand for inclusion or transformation, a narrow focus on surgical intervention limits the ability of public institutions to meaningfully redress the exclusion of transgender people. What happens in the process is that gender affirming care, including surgery, comes to stand for a broader desire for inclusion and a more radical transformation of society that cannot be articulated in clinical or legal discourse. While people like Vitória and Laura were able to access gender affirming surgery, the state failed to address their social vulnerability, in ways that were made invisible, in Vitória's case, or pathologized, when, in Laura's case, health professionals wondered whether Laura desired, "too much." Yet Vitória and Laura both point to the ordinary forms of care and diverse projects of transformation that may emerge from expanded access to health technology secured through right-to-health litigation.

In the final ruling on the class action, Ellen Gracie of the Supreme Federal Tribunal temporarily suspended the decision by Judge Rios's court, saying that although transgender people "merit the full respect of Brazilian society and the Judiciary," owing to the "suffering and hard realities of transsexuals," the court could not order the executive branch of government to change its policy by including a new procedure in the public health system (Ventura 2011). This is part of an ongoing debate in Brazil about the power of courts to make decisions about the right to health in general and not on an individual basis. Although not compelled by a court, the Ministry of Health accepted the logic of the *ação civil pública* and approved access to gender affirming care before the case could be heard by the entire Supreme Federal Tribunal.

Patients such as the ones I worked with were granted a minimum of services deemed medically necessary; other care, such as breast augmentation or facial hair removal, which might have been socially much more significant, was deemed cosmetic. However, the quotidian practices of transformation of transgender subjects like Vitória and Laura point to the vital potential of access to care, even within a neoliberal framework. Subjectivity is a distinct field of self-authorship, not fully determined by the state or the market, and it must be attended to on its own terms.

Transformation may be an object of desire or a proxy for another desire. Michelle, another patient, told me in the days after her genital surgery that it "isn't the thousand wonders they said it would be." When I met her a year earlier, she told me that her hopes for the surgery were to "set everything right." Reflecting on her own struggles, Michelle told me, "Life isn't always a brightly colored rainbow. So, in the midst of darkness, we have to find ourselves."

Claims to transgender rights tenuously link trajectories of individual transformation with macro processes of social transformation, which in turn provide the conditions for articulating personal and intimate experiences. Surgery here is both a metaphor and a concrete basis for imagining different life possibilities and social worlds. When I spoke to Michelle a year after her surgery, months after she expressed her disappointment and frustration to me, she was extremely happy, and seemed almost to be a different person:

> On the day of my surgery, I went alone . . . I was apprehensive—what would happen? And it was good, even, that I had gone alone, and remained alone, thinking about what I was doing. The decisions that we make in life are very important, and in order for them to be valid, one cannot give up in the middle of

the journey. There are those that give up when they have already set foot in the surgical service. But then, I went, I wanted it, and now I am here.

These transgender subjects do transform their lives even in the face of stigma and within the impossible confines of a biopolitical discourse that renders their existence precarious. The expanded access to care made possible by the judicialization of the right to health is not a world-changing event, but it does open a space for trans people's desire to transform local social worlds and initiate new lines of belonging.

Joshua Franklin is an MD/PhD student in anthropology at the University of Pennsylvania. Franklin's research interests include gender and sexuality, mental health, and Brazil. Currently, Franklin is beginning a project to explore the impact of care and role of medical institutions in the lives of transgender and gender-nonconforming young people in Philadelphia.

Acknowledgements

I would like to gratefully acknowledge João Biehl, Adriana Petryna, and Alex Gertner for their wonderful guidance. I would also like to thank the medical anthropology writing group at the University of Pennsylvania, the editors of this issue of *TSQ*, and the anonymous peer reviewers for their insightful comments. All translations from Portuguese to English are my own. This research was supported by grants from the Fulbright US Student Program and the Brazilian Studies Association.

Notes

1. Fieldwork was conducted for five months in 2009 and 2010 and nine months in 2012. Thirty-three trans women and seven trans men participated in my study, in the form of interviews and observations gathered at the clinic. I followed the trajectories of five trans women and two trans men in more depth through home visits and extended interviews. Of these participants, while a few were employed as health or education professionals, the majority were unemployed, engaged in informal work such as sex work, or employed in low-wage occupations. All names have been changed.

2. In this article, I focus on inequality based on class more than race. I did not observe the same salience of racialized inequalities that Jarrín (2015), for example, describes. In part, this is because my study was conducted in Porto Alegre in southern Brazil, where a far greater proportion of the population identifies as white relative to Brazil as a whole. The intersections of race- and class-based structures for transgender people throughout Brazil are an important area for further research.

3. The notion that trans identities can be formulated as a set of diagnostic criteria is deeply problematic. My goal here is not to examine the pathologization of trans identities or the politics of psychiatric diagnosis but to draw attention to the complex negotiation that occurs in clinical practice.

References

Arán, Márcia, and Daniela Murta. 2009. "Do diagnóstico de transtorno de identidade de gênero às redescrições da experiência da transexualidade: Uma reflexão sobre gênero, tecnologia e saúde" ("From the Diagnosis of Gender Identity Disorder to the Redescription of the Experience of Transsexuality: A Reflection on Gender, Technology, and Health"). *Physis: Revista de Saúde Coletiva* (*Physis: Journal of Public Health*) 19, no. 1: 15–41.

Associated Press. 2007. "Brazil: Free Sex Change Operations." *New York Times*, August 18.

Bento, Berenice. 2006. *A reinvenção do corpo: Sexualidade e gênero na experiência transsexual* (*The Reinvention of the Body: Sexuality and Gender in the Transsexual Experience*). Rio de Janeiro: Garamond.

Berlant, Lauren. 2011. *Cruel Optimism*. Durham, NC: Duke University Press.

Berlant, Lauren, and Jay Prosser. 2011. "Life Writing and Intimate Publics: A Conversation with Lauren Berlant." *Biography* 34, no. 1: 180–87.

Biehl, João. 2013. "The Judicialization of Biopolitics: Claiming the Right to Pharmaceuticals in Brazilian Courts." *American Ethnologist* 40, no. 3: 419–36.

Biehl, João, Mariana Socal, and Joseph J. Amon. 2016. "The Judicialization of Health and the Quest for State Accountability: Evidence from 1,262 Lawsuits for Access to Medicines in Southern Brazil." *Health and Human Rights* 18, no. 1: 209–20.

da Silva, Virgílio Afonso, and Fernanda Vargas Terrazas. 2011. "Claiming the Right to Health in Brazilian Courts: The Exclusion of the Already Excluded?" *Law and Social Inquiry* 36, no. 4: 825–53.

Edmonds, Alexander. 2010. *Pretty Modern: Beauty, Sex, and Plastic Surgery in Brazil*. Durham, NC: Duke University Press.

Ferraz, Octavio L. M. 2011. "Harming the Poor through Social Rights Litigation: Lessons from Brazil." *South Texas Law Review* 89, no. 7: 1643–68.

Irving, Dan. 2008. "Normalized Transgressions: Legitimizing the Transgender Body as Productive." *Radical History Review*, no. 100: 38–59.

Jarrín, Alvaro. 2015. "Towards a Biopolitics of Beauty: Eugenics, Aesthetic Hierarchies, and Plastic Surgery in Brazil." *Journal of Latin American Cultural Studies* 24, no. 4: 535–52.

———. 2016. "Untranslatable Subjects: Travesti Access to Public Healthcare in Brazil." *TSQ* 3, nos. 3–4: 357–75.

Kulick, Don. 1998. *Travesti: Sex, Gender, and Culture among Brazilian Transgendered Prostitutes*. Chicago: University of Chicago Press.

Metzl, Jonathan M., and Helena Hansen. 2014. "Structural Competency: Theorizing a New Medical Engagement with Stigma and Inequality." *Social Science and Medicine* 103: 126–33.

Salamon, Gayle. 2010. *Assuming a Body: Transgender and Rhetorics of Materiality*. New York: Columbia University Press.

Silva, Joseli Maria, and Paulo Jorge Viera. 2014. "Geographies of Sexualities in Brazil: Between National Invisibility and Subordinate Inclusion in Postcolonial Networks of Knowledge Production." *Geography Compass* 8, no. 10: 767–77.

Spade, Dean. 2011. *Normal Life: Administrative Violence, Critical Trans Politics, and the Limits of the Law*. Cambridge, MA: South End.

Stewart, Kathleen. 2007. *Ordinary Affects*. Durham, NC: Duke University Press.

Teixeira, Flavia B. 2011. "Não basta abrir a janela . . . Reflexões sobre alguns efeitos dos discursos médico e jurídico nas (in)definições da transexualidade" ("It's Not Enough to Open the Window . . . Reflections on Some Effects of Medical and Juridical Discourse on the

(In)definitions of Transsexuality"). *Anuário antropológico* (*Anthropological Annual*) 2011, no. 1: 127–60.

Towle, Evan B., and Lynn M. Morgan. 2006. "Romancing the Transgender Native: Rethinking the Use of the 'Third Gender' Concept." In *Transgender Studies Reader*, edited by Susan Stryker and Stephen Whittle, 666–84. New York: Routledge.

Valentine, David. 2007. *Imagining Transgender: An Ethnography of a Category*. Durham, NC: Duke University Press.

Ventura, Miriam. 2011. *A Transexualidade no Tribunal: Saúde e cidadania* (*Transsexuality in the Courts: Health and Citizenship*). Rio de Janeiro: Editora da Universidade do Estado do Rio de Janeiro.

West, Isaac. 2014. *Transforming Citizenships: Transgender Articulations of the Law*. New York: New York University Press.

"We Are Here to Help"

Who Opens the Gate for Surgeries?

RIKI LANE

Abstract Many trans and gender-diverse (TGD) people seek surgeries to align their bodies with their gender identity. This contested field has historically been dominated by mental health professionals, whom TGD people have often seen as "gatekeepers." Gaining access to medical treatments, while avoiding pathologization and stigmatization, is the central dilemma of TGD clients' relationship with clinicians. For clinicians, the dilemma is inverted—they seek to provide access to treatment but also to mitigate risks of harm to their clients and of legal action if clients regret surgery. In prominent cases, two former clients who regretted their surgeries sued the Monash Health Gender Clinic, precipitating a review of operations and a three-month closure. Internationally and in Australia, the approach to care has moved from psychiatric dominance toward a collaborative approach between clients and clinicians from varied disciplines to achieve the best individual outcome. This shift is partially reflected in changes to diagnostic criteria and clinical guidelines. These changes have increased access to treatments for many TGD people previously excluded. However, at this clinic, surgeons' requirements for approval by a mental health professional have changed little in forty years. This article provides a clear exposition of how clinicians in the most prominent Australian gender clinic approach approval of medical treatment. Clinicians have moved to depathologize their approach, but the tensions defining the clinician-client relationship remain in balance: the risks of regret after treatment versus self-harm without it; and access for clients' desired treatments versus medico-legal risk for the clinician.

Keywords trans and gender diverse, health, gatekeeping, collaboration, diagnostic criteria

Introduction

Many trans and gender-diverse (TGD)[1] people seek access to psychotherapeutic, hormonal, and surgical treatments but wish to avoid pathologization and stigmatization. This conflict is the central dilemma of their relationship with clinicians, particularly mental health professionals (MHPs). For clinicians, the dilemma is inverted—they seek to provide access to treatment but also to mitigate risks of harm to their clients and of legal action if clients regret surgery. These tensions underlie contention around different approaches to clinical practice and gender variance.

TSQ: Transgender Studies Quarterly ★ Volume 5, Number 2 ★ May 2018 **207**
DOI 10.1215/23289252-4348648 © 2018 Duke University Press

As I cover elsewhere (Lane 2012), client-clinician relationships, in general, have shifted toward ones in which autonomous clients actively organize their health, while medical practitioners retain regulated powers to authorize treatments (Rogers and Pilgrim 2005). Within that frame, psychiatric professionals have historically defended their professional dominance over treatment of gender variance from other professions and TGD clients, centrally by maintaining the mental illness diagnosis (Jaarsma and Welin 2012).

Sociological analyses of psychiatry place differing emphases on imposition and consent (Rogers and Pilgrim 2005: 130–32). This dynamic differs between people who voluntarily seek psychotherapy and those with severe psychiatric diagnoses who may actively avoid treatment. TGD people often experience both consent and imposition. They consensually approach MHPs like the first group, not perceiving gender variance as a mental health issue. However, when seeking approval for medical procedures, they are treated like the second group, having to accept an imposed psychiatric diagnosis and limited treatment options.

Another key sociological issue is around power in the clinician-client relationship. Maintenance of psychiatric dominance over TGD health care (Willis 1983; Rogers and Pilgrim 2005) requires, first, that gender variance continue to be *medicalized* as a condition needing medical diagnosis and treatment, and second, that it be *psycho-pathologized*, requiring mental health diagnosis and treatment. Psychiatric dominance is challenged by increasing case management by gender specialists other than MHPs. Like other groups receiving mental health diagnoses (Corrigan 2005), TGD people resist stigmatization in clinical interactions and have built their own social movements focused on *depsycho-pathologization*.

As outlined in the sociology of diagnosis, battles over diagnosis work at multiple levels: in global political and economic agendas, organizationally in interprofessional relations, and in social interactions between clients and professionals (Jutel and Nettleton 2011: 799). TGD people face a dilemma similar to that of some other client groups. A medical diagnosis confers benefits: a coherent explanation, social legitimacy, and access to medical treatments and health insurance coverage. However, there are the downsides of pathologization and stigmatization, especially for psychiatric diagnoses. TGD people rely on medicine and psychiatry for treatment, yet they question the pathologizing discourses and stigmatizing practices. This tension between seeking approval for treatment and resisting pathologization is a defining characteristic of the relationship between clinicians and TGD people, both as individuals and as a social movement.

From Gatekeeping to Collaboration

There is an ongoing paradigm shift from the gatekeeping model to the collaborative model (Lev 2004) of TGD health care. The decrease in psychiatric power is illustrated by TGD activism influencing treatment modalities, the increased numbers of clinicians who are TGD, and the declining influence of explicitly pathologizing "old guard" clinicians. Many new, trans-affirmative clinicians have emerged: over one thousand people attended the 2016 World Professional Association for Transgender Heath (WPATH) symposium.

Many TGD people and clinicians argued for moving TGD health care out of psychiatry—leading to the replacement of the gender identity disorder diagnosis in the American Psychiatric Association's (APA) *Diagnostic and Statistical Manual* (*DSM*) with the less pathologizing gender dysphoria in *DSM*-5 (APA 2013). The gender incongruence diagnosis, located in a non–mental health section of the World Health Organization's International Classification of Diseases version 11 (ICD-11), is undergoing field trials (Robles et al. 2016). There has been considerable controversy around these diagnoses (De Cuypere and Winter 2016; Drescher, Cohen-Kettenis, and Reed 2016), reflecting the competing global agendas and interprofessional tensions. WPATH's *Standards of Care* version 7 (*SOC*-7) (Coleman et al. 2012) adopted a more trans-affirmative approach, likely to be strengthened in *SOC*-8.

In classic gatekeeping model, the MHP restricted access to the indivisible package of surgical and hormonal treatment known as sex reassignment surgery (SRS) to people who met strict pathological and psychiatric diagnostic criteria. In the collaborative model, the clinician and client together determine the most appropriate gender outcome, including varied combinations of gender affirming treatments.

The gatekeeping model was established by 1980 and codified in the *SOC* (Fraser and Knudson 2017). In this model, several months of psychiatric assessment led to a diagnosis and a letter authorizing hormones, and twelve months of "real life experience" in the "other gender" led to a letter authorizing surgery. The psychiatrist's letters constituted the "obligatory passage point" (Epstein 1996: 15), which all candidates for SRS had to negotiate. The *DSM* and *SOC* institutionalized the view of gender variance as a psychological disorder and constructed the defining tension in the clinical relationship between access (to treatment and insurance coverage) and pathologization.

In the collaborative model, developing since the 1990s, a clinician accepts the TGD person's sense of gender, respects their decision-making capacity, and facilitates transition to another gender position (Kirk and Kulkarni 2006). The shifts include movement from psychiatric dominance to multidisciplinarity, from access to SRS as a one-size-fits-all treatment for certified transsexuals to individually negotiated treatment options, and from gender as binary to spectrum.

Debates

In the limited relevant social science and health literature, there are ongoing debates about diagnoses and approval processes for medical treatments (Lev

2013; Selvaggi and Giordano 2014), and around how progressive the recent changes have been (Dewey and Gesbeck 2015). I'll briefly mention three key arguments. Jodie Dewey and Melissa Gesbeck (2015: 41) argue that "the seemingly progressive changes to the recent *DSM*-5 and *SOC*-7 may not be enough to alter the underlying structure of social control and power that diagnostic categories have over trans people, but rather work to further deepen and normalize non-normative gender expressions as deviant and pathological." By contrast, W. P. Bouman et al. (2014: 383) accept that *SOC*-7 can be seen to perpetuate gate-keeping and a paternalist attitude but point out that "in several cases, TGD people have indeed not taken this type of responsibility [for their choices] as they have litigated against clinicians who have provided them with treatments they have previously sought and have later come to regret." Stephanie Budge and lore m dickey (2017: 10) outline principles that clinicians should follow: avoid diagnosis where possible; make it clear that gender variance is not a disorder; discuss with the client the psychological effect of making a diagnosis, for example, in a surgery approval letter; and consult with the client about reasons for delays due to co-occurring disorders.

Monash Health's Gender Clinic (GC) in Australia acts as a microcosm for how such debates have played out in practice. There are few gender clinics and practitioners in the field in Australia, especially surgeons, and the vast majority are in private practice. While the experiences at this one clinic are of course not generalizable, they have relevance to other jurisdictions. In particular, they high-light that despite large changes in guidelines and diagnostic criteria, the central dilemmas remain: for TGD people, how to seek access to medical treatments while avoiding psycho-pathologization, and for clinicians, how to provide access to desired treatments while avoiding harm to clients and medico-legal risk.

Methods

My research project aims to inform the development of the GC's model of care and of WPATH's *SOC*-8. As this article focuses on surgery, relevant research objectives include documenting (1) current approaches to decisions to approve medical treatments by GC clinicians, and (2) how approaches have changed, in light of shifting models of care. The overall approach is a sociology of science and medicine, seeking to understand the changes in clinical diagnostic and approval processes in the interaction between clinicians, TGD people, and the broader society. Within that framework, this article concentrates on providing an expo-sition of how the clinicians see the changes, rather than on theoretical explanation and positioning.

The method used is standard social science thematic analysis of relevant biomedical and social science literature, interviews with clinicians, and obser-vation of clinical review meetings.

A literature review examined approaches and criteria for approval of TGD surgeries. This focused on the key guidelines for diagnosis (*DSM*, ICD) and clinical treatment (*SOC*), and shifts in treatment approaches over the last fifteen years. An initial search performed in my EndNote database used search terms with Boolean operators such as "surgery AND approval OR regret OR criteria"; this was supplemented by searches of relevant databases for biomedicine and social science and in Google Scholar. Articles were selected by relevance and recency (last fifteen years). Analysis identified key themes.

Qualitative interviews were conducted with members of the GC clinical review group, guided by a written schedule. Analysis proceeded by thematic coding, initially according to interview schedule questions informed by the literature, and subsequently by those that arose in the interviews. Interview and observation material was sorted into themes and rearranged under broad headings for reporting.

Potential participants were members of the GC clinical review team, from across a range of clinical disciplines with varying interactions with TGD clients. The study was described at a review team meeting, and participants were invited face-to-face and via e-mail. Written consent was gained, and participants were asked if they were willing to be identified. They were sent interview transcripts to check, amend, and clarify via e-mail exchanges. Surnames are used for identified participants, first-name pseudonyms for unidentified participants.

Eight clinicians were approached, and seven were interviewed in early 2017. In addition, coinvestigator and GC Clinical Director Jaco Erasmus participated in a pilot interview, which shaped authorial descriptions. The participants are

- Harjit Bagga, GC clinical psychologist since 2010;
- Simon Ceber, gender surgeon 1976–2016;
- Jaco Erasmus, GC psychiatrist since 2009, clinical director since 2016;
- Fintan Harte, psychiatrist, TGD clients since 1990s, with GC during 2000–2015, clinical director during 2009–15;
- Andrew Ives, gender surgeon since 2010;
- Rafaella Karas, a new clinical psychologist;
- Georgia Dacakis, a speech therapist associated with the clinic since 1980; and
- "Catherine," a psychiatrist consulting with the GC since 2013.

The Monash Health Human Research Ethics Committee approved the project.

I am employed as a GC project/research worker, with considerable contact with GC MHPs. Contact with the external psychiatrists, speech pathologist, and surgeons is via the review committee and the Australia New Zealand Professional Association for Transgender Health (ANZPATH). Due to my embedded position at the GC, participants were probably more open in their comments than with an external researcher. However, I have felt a responsibility to present participants' views and the organization in a constructive manner.

Results

Themes arising from analysis are organized under the following headings: history of the clinic, GC processes now, clinical review meetings, guidelines and practices, and surgeons' requirements.

History of the Clinic

Australian TGD health care follows international trends, shaped by local health system context and gender clinic history. The overall health-care system is a public/private mix, providing free treatment in public hospitals, with often lengthy waiting lists. Primary care is overwhelmingly private, with a government health insurance scheme (Medicare) providing reimbursement of fees, accepted by doctors as full payment for 85 percent of services. Private health insurance covers some private allied health and hospital costs, allowing avoidance of public hospital waiting lists. However, as TGD surgeries are not currently available in public hospitals (except occasional chest or internal genitalia surgeries), significant costs are incurred for private health insurance and procedures—the GC provides financial assistance to its clients.

Access to prescriptions and specialist services are strongly gatekept by the medical profession, with limited referral and prescribing rights for other health professionals. To access insurance payments for allied health and medical specialists, referral is required from a general practitioner (GP), similar to a family physician in North America.

Gender-affirmation surgeries were first performed in Melbourne, Australia, in the 1960s. A gender dysphoria team developed in the 1970s, and the current Gender Clinic[2] at Monash Health is the direct descendent of this team, with several original members still participating. It is the most prominent Australian gender clinic, with the most substantial public funding.

Simon Ceber, Georgia Dacakis, and Fintan Harte described the early days.

CEBER: [In] 1976 . . . [Gynecology] Prof. Walters had a patient who he felt needed gender reassignment. . . . He asked the head of the plastic surgery unit . . . and I was her assistant. . . . It worked out all right. . . . We had a second one within a couple of months and word got out through the grapevine . . . this was going to be an ongoing scene, so a committee was established.

The team had a broader composition then, including the hospital head nurse, a Catholic priest, and a lawyer, in addition to the current membership of surgeons, endocrinologist, psychiatrists, psychologists, and social worker. Notably, "it wasn't a mental health person in charge of the team. It was a gynecologist," said Dacakis.

From 1979, they followed the Harry Benjamin Standards of Care (HBIGDA 1985), which provided some medico-legal protection.

> CEBER: It was two years of real life, a fairly strict criteria . . . not fundamentally different than now, except the durations might be a bit different, but free of major psychiatric disorder and able to give informed consent.

The guidelines focused on "that it was irreversible surgery, and therefore you had to tread very carefully" (Dacakis). While overall, processes were similar, "there was a lot more caution about approving people for surgery" (Dacakis). There was strong perception of their gatekeeper role.

> DACAKIS: People had to prove that they were living in the female role for a set period [and] the *SOC* even suggested that they have someone else confirm this. If a case was considered complex, then individuals were invited to come and present to the team. I'm sure they truly felt as though they were facing the gatekeeper!

In an example of classic gatekeeping, many people were refused treatments—due to age, presentation, or fetishism—who would now be accepted. Clinicians looked back with some regret.

> HARTE: Being over sixty used to be an exclusion criteria. . . . It's great to see them reappear: [they] have marked improved quality of life because of the surgery.

> CEBER: One patient age about sixty-five was refused repeatedly who came to see me age seventy-five still wanting the operation. She was very fit and I would have been happy to do it . . . today.

> DACAKIS: A couple of decisions were based on factors that now would have no bearing. . . . I deferred to the psychiatrists. . . . An older woman [was] not approved for surgery because of her age and . . . "inappropriate" dress that attracted attention. I felt . . . she should have been approved for surgery. . . . I should have supported her application more. . . . I still sometimes worry about how she dealt with that outcome.

The team worked semisecretively, due to disapproval from other health professionals. After hospital mergers in 1987 they moved to the new Monash Health network. After ten years there with public funding, surgeries shifted to a private hospital.

> CEBER: Most other surgeons [at Monash] looked on it as some sort of disgraceful surgery, and the nursing staff similarly weren't very friendly. They weren't very nice to the patients either.

Former clients who detransitioned after surgeries sued the GC in 2004 and 2009, backed by conservative Christian groups. Although unsuccessful in court, these cases precipitated government enquiries and the temporary closure of the clinic in 2009, resulting in a new clinical director, revamped assessment protocols, and a modest funding increase. This pivotal experience led to much stricter adherence to *SOC/DSM* clinical guidelines.

The team meetings reviewed all cases, especially when the psychiatrist was about to write letters to approve treatment. Discussing the team's role, Ceber argued that deficiencies allowed approvals for the people who sued the GC, who may not have met diagnostic criteria.

> CEBER: It was . . . more loose, more dependent on individual psychiatrist's feelings. They would ignore psychologists. . . . It didn't feel as tight and that's when we got into trouble.

Until 2016, the GC had extremely limited funding: psychiatrists worked two afternoons per week to assess clients under *DSM* diagnostic criteria and thus approve medical treatment. A social worker provided limited psycho-social support, and a clinical psychologist investigated complexities such as cognitive difficulties or psychiatric conditions. Some funding subsidized private surgeries and free voice services at La Trobe University. GC psychiatrists also saw gender clients privately. From 2016, clinical psychologists, trained by GC psychiatrists, began to do assessments within the GC and privately.

In 2016, the Victorian state government increased funding six-fold, allowing greatly enhanced access: expanded personnel and therapeutic support, reduced waiting times, increased funding for private surgeries, and moves toward public provision of surgical and other services. The GC now aims to provide a "one-stop shop . . . publicly funded [for] anybody who needs a free service" (Bagga). In the developing model of care, more services will be provided in primary care. The GC will take more complex cases and provide statewide specialist support and education and referral services, using tele-health in remote areas.

The GC is envisioned to be a center of excellence that will develop up-to-date TGD health care, provide excellent clinical service, expand therapeutic and social support, and explore new treatment modalities. It aims to be a great teaching facility and to pursue research with university and international collaboration.

GC Processes Now

All clinicians agree with depsycho-pathologization, that gender variance is not a mental health disorder but a healthy natural variation. However, the TGD population has high rates of depression, anxiety, and suicidality (Smith et al. 2014), largely caused by stigmatization and social exclusion (Robles et al. 2016).

Client experience at the GC begins with GP or specialist medical practitioner referrals. Following *SOC*-7 guidelines, GC MHPs undertake at least three sessions to assess client goals and desired medical treatments (if any), psychiatric history, mental state, *DSM* diagnostic criteria for gender dysphoria, social circumstances, and so forth. If there are no complexities needing investigation, and the client is seeking medical treatment, a letter will be written to a hormone prescriber and/or for chest surgery. After the client has spent a period of time on hormones, an additional assessment will result in a letter approving internal and/or external genital surgeries.

Routine versus Complex Cases. Many straightforward cases are now assessed by private psychologists. Participants agreed that "routine" cases did not always need an MHP assessment, but that it was usually valuable.

The GC sees many clients with more complex issues such as psychiatric disorders like psychosis, dissociation, or autism; intellectual disability; history of trauma; unstable social circumstances; homelessness; and substance abuse. These clients are referred by GPs or private MHPs, and they take considerably more sessions.

A different complexity is increasingly seen with clients who present as nonbinary or gender fluid. The *SOC* gives little guidance (Fraser and Knudson 2017), and clinicians lack expertise with these clients, who often face more difficult social issues than those undertaking a binary transition.

All MHPs expected that increasing numbers of TGD people will seek approval for hormones and potentially some surgeries from experienced GPs rather than MHPs. However, this does not remove the gatekeeping function—the authority to say no—but shifts it from MHPs to GPs. For general medical conditions in Australia, GPs usually approve prescriptions but refer to a specialist for surgical decisions. As discussed later, Australian surgeons require MHP assessments for TGD surgeries.

Informed Consent. A great variety of approaches are included in informed consent models of TGD health care, mainly for hormones (Deutsch 2012). Movement toward such models has been more cautious in Australia than in the United States. For any general procedure, doctors would say they practice informed consent, which does not equal treatment on demand. GC clinicians and ANZPATH recently accepted the Equinox Clinic model in which an experienced GP would make a mental health assessment and refer more complex cases. However, they did not accept a model in which "somebody . . . look[s] at a video . . . and after fifteen minutes . . . [they] sign the consent form, and go off with a prescription" (Harte). Where there are complexities, Bagga commented, "I get really concerned about that poor GP having to manage it."

MHPs agreed that *SOC*-8 would need much greater clarity on informed consent models. Harte thought that ICD-11 could take gender variance out of psychiatry.

> HARTE: [Had] endocrinologists like Harry Benjamin dominated the field in the 1960s [rather than psychiatrists] . . . this could well have been . . . in ICD under endocrinology, and mental health would be on the periphery. Perhaps we are seeing a shift back to that.

Dispelling Gatekeeping Expectations. Building a therapeutic alliance with clients can be complicated by the clinician's dual role as assessor and therapist, creating a power imbalance (Fraser and Knudson 2017: 23).

> KARAS: Some individuals have been more guarded, [having] a history of relational trauma, or . . . abuse, or . . . disrupted attachment. . . . It takes a while to build trust. . . . Once you let them know that you're not there to make a judgement, but are rather interested about . . . their journey, often a lot of the guardedness . . . drops.

At the GC and in private practice, many clients bring strong expectations of gatekeeping. A common strategy was to try to dispel these in the first session. While some clients were very clear that they only wanted to get their approval letters, many valued the therapeutic experience.

> HARTE: I say . . . "My job is not to say whether you can or cannot have hormones or surgery, that's your decision. My job is to help you make an informed decision." At the end, . . . they'll either . . . say "I've found it really helpful" or "it's been a complete and utter waste of time and money."
>
> About ten years ago, I started to say "I'm not a gatekeeper, and if you want to see me as a gatekeeper, I'm there to open the gate, [which] I do the vast majority of the time." . . . A lot of trans people would say "I really like the gatekeeper that holds open the gate."

Similarly, Andrew Ives cited a surgeon's conference presentation that responded to patient complaints, noting the surgeon's comment: "'You know what? We're actually here to help you.'"

IVES: I am trying to help people achieve what they want, [not] put things in their way by saying "I go by the standards." I walk a line between being a responsible, ethical, and moral surgeon and . . . trying to . . . help people.

Clinicians stressed the value of the assessment process, even for those with no mental health problems. Once a professional has confirmed that they are not "crazy," some clients say they are able to convince their family that their issues are real. It also allows TGD people a space to "really have a narrative about what was actually going on. It wasn't something that they would openly be able to discuss with their parents, or their friends" (Karas).

Clinical Review Meetings

In 2016 the team meetings morphed into two: weekly and bimonthly. The weekly internal meeting is a clinical review by GC MHPs, sharing perspectives and difficulties, especially for new psychologists. This group considers hormone approvals, with psychologists bringing cases "to get psychiatrist sign-off" (Bagga). The bimonthly meeting, which also includes surgeons, endocrinologist, a speech pathologist, and external private psychiatrists, considers surgical approvals and applications for financial assistance. Participants objected to my labeling the meetings a review "committee," saying that they were standard clinical review team meetings.

Whereas the surgery review meeting originally made decisions on approvals, now it mainly ensures that paperwork is correct. Prior to approval, MHPs may seek advice on diagnosis and management. Once they have written the letter, approval is finished: the meeting checks that everyone is aware of any client needs for extra support, and so on.

CEBER: [Better] that all cases, even simple, do get discussed. That's how you get experience.

HARTE: [Before] a totally irreversible surgical procedure, it is worthwhile having all key stakeholders in the room to make sure that everybody is happy and . . . all the documentation is there.

All clinicians valued the chance to have a face-to-face interdisciplinary meeting, to foster collegiality.

BAGGA: You don't get those collegial relationships with external service providers anywhere else. I wouldn't have contact with the surgeons.

IVES: In the private world, it's very insular. You are there by yourself, see . . . your own patient list. Same time every week . . . the same staff, the same people doing their lists. . . . So, you develop a very closeted world as a surgeon.

My other interest [is] in burns. . . . [In] any complex clinical area, the multidisciplinary team is the way. . . . Nothing beats sitting down with a group of varied clinical workers to discuss cases.

So in both the gender clinic work and his burns work, Ives emphasized the importance of participating in a multidisciplinary team, face-to-face. Ives continued, "If you have just one person, what if that person is a rogue element? . . . At some stage they're going to operate on someone who they [shouldn't]. That brings a detriment . . . for people who are trying to work in an ethical, moral, and professional manner."

Psychologists spoke little at the surgery review group—many were new, but as Karas argued: "It feels like a very medical framework . . . [psychiatrists] getting opinions from the medical professionals. I'm hoping [for] a more holistic approach." That multidisciplinary approach may develop as newer staff develop confidence.

Not a "Committee Deciding People's Fate." Many TGD people see the idea that individual cases are reviewed by a committee as highly problematic. MHPs said they bring their concerns and doubts to the review meeting, but prior to approval being made.

HARTE: [People are not] reviewed after having been told they would get surgery. . . . It would be frightening to the community to think that there is this meeting of people that are deciding their fate. . . . They need some reassurance.

As a speech pathologist, Dacakis does not sign approval letters, but she still felt disapproval from the TGD community.

DACAKIS: There is still a feeling . . . that the team acts a gatekeeper. . . . That perception caused a lot of trauma. . . . I don't feel from my insider perspective that there is anywhere near the behavior considered as gatekeeping. . . . I feel sad that there is still some of that feeling within the community. I don't feel I could say, "Hey listen. It's really not like that," without community members saying, "You're on the other side and there's a power imbalance."

This goes back to the central dilemma: there *is still a power imbalance*. While MHPs' approach has changed and they no longer position themselves as the decision makers, they remain the ones who can approve, delay, or deny treatments.

Guidelines and Practices

Debates on gatekeeping focus on the *SOC* guidelines and *DSM* criteria, around which global political agendas clash, with tensions between institutions (APA, WHO, WPATH), health professions, and TGD activism. This section describes how the clinicians view and use these guidelines.

Provide Client Access and Protect Clinician. All participants said they follow the *SOC* and *DSM*, altering their approach as these change. However, despite the many amendments, the underlying purpose remains the same—to enable access to treatments for TGD people, while protecting clinicians from medico-legal risk.

Diagnosis is now regarded as mostly irrelevant to the client's journey. Rather than directly diagnosing someone with gender dysphoria in word or print, MHPs write approval letters that state, "Based on current diagnostic manuals, this person fulfills criteria for a diagnosis," and they protect themselves legally by recording that they follow recognized guidelines.

> HARTE: Since 1979 [*SOC* had] two aspects . . . (1) to inform clinicians on best practice . . . (2) to protect doctors in . . . a very hostile professional environment. [At first] it was two psychiatrists, then . . . a psychiatrist and a psychologist, then MHPs. So, . . . watering down required qualifications.

While Bagga, a psychologist, felt the need for safeguards to "protect people and professionals, [as] surgery [can] go really horribly wrong," Catherine, a psychiatrist, downplayed medico-legal considerations: "It's always a risk to any medical practitioner, but not overly so in this group."

Participants said there have always been both gatekeeping and collaborative aspects. While the client has autonomy to decide what they wish to do with their life, the clinician has autonomy to decide whether to support those choices.

> BAGGA: Collaboration is much greater [now]. But it's still a bit slow. . . . Unfortunately. . . . It's still gatekeepery, but slightly less.

> KARAS: We do make decisions about what will happen for this individual. . . . You try to get collaboration. . . . But, you are there to provide a service . . . to make observations and give something back.

Rarely a "No" but a "Not Yet." Very few people are now excluded by the diagnostic criteria—it is very rarely a "no" but a "not yet." This shifted as *DSM* criteria broadened and *SOC* guidelines focused more on distress than diagnosis. Rather than seeing their job as giving approval, MHPs mentioned other tasks: assessing whether a client meets requirements under guidelines, ensuring that a client's decision-making process is sound and not influenced by medical conditions, and making sure that there is good understanding of planned procedures and consequences. Reasons to delay treatment include clinician investigations of capacity to consent or broader identity disturbances such as autism; referrals to other medical professionals to stabilize active psychosis or address medical contraindications; referrals to social workers and peer support groups to assist in stabilizing the social situation and addressing lack of social supports; and allowing time for client actions to address medical (e.g., extreme obesity), psychiatric (e.g., active psychosis), and social (e.g., homelessness) contraindications for surgery.

Having a mental health condition no longer excludes surgery approval, once stabilized.

> HARTE: When I started, the number of contraindications were fairly extensive, . . . they're limited now, [although] *SOC-7* clearly states that somebody who is actively psychotic is not suitable to undergo medical treatments.

> BAGGA: That's one of the big changes, people can come in now with mental health concerns and we're not going to say no.

People are no longer ruled ineligible because of a *DSM* transvestic fetishism diagnosis.

> HARTE: No, absolutely not. In fact it's very common to have some sort of sexual arousal association with cross-dressing at varying stages.

While not pathologizing fetishistic behaviors, MHPs still had concerns. If a birth-assigned male client was currently strongly motivated by sexual elements of transition, they were likely to regret hormone therapy, as estrogen will usually reduce or eliminate their sex drive.

There also were concerns about general identity issues, of which gender dysphoria is one aspect.

> BAGGA: We're seeing a lot more younger people . . . with not only gender variance but broader identity disturbance. That's one of the tricky parts, one of the diagnostic dilemmas.

In the rare cases in which clinicians say no to surgery, it is usually because of alternate diagnoses such as severe autism or medical complications including obesity: "It's a big operation [with] significant risks, and I'm not willing to put someone in danger . . . just to get paid" (Ives).

Some psychologists were concerned that the push for depathologization may have led to the criteria for approving treatment to be too loose, thus limiting the clinician's ability to say no, while a psychiatrist saw it as allowing more flexibility:

> KARAS: It shouldn't just be a checklist "You meet *SOC-7, DSM-5* criteria . . . go ahead." There needs to be a little bit more thinking about the psychology of that individual.

> BAGGA: [*DSM* and *SOC*] make it trickier . . . when somebody . . . technically meets these criteria because they're so broad. It makes it really hard to say no . . . when you've got real concerns about their safety, adjustment, and resilience. . . . I feel like I've got my hands tied.

> CATHERINE: *DSM-5* has broadened things and we have a little bit more flexibility.

"First, Do No Harm."   There was acute awareness that not treating can cause harm. This caused considerable internal struggle for the MHPs; for example, in one case a client self-harmed after the clinician asked to further explore some issues:

> HARTE: A lot of clinicians misinterpret ["first do no harm"] as "If in doubt, do nothing" because not doing anything can do an awful lot of harm.

> IVES: One could argue that . . . by not operating . . . , you're doing more harm [given] the suicide rate, or self-harm rate in patients who are denied . . . or can't undergo surgery.

MHPs sought to ensure that any risks were addressed—often entailing some delay in approving treatments. All clinicians worked to ensure they did not invalidate their clients in sessions, seeing that as a major source of possible harm. Concern about potential harm increased with the irreversibility of treatments; hormone blockers were the least worrisome, followed by feminizing hormones, masculinizing hormones, chest surgeries, and genital surgeries, which presented the most concern:

> BAGGA: Surgery, it just feels like it's so final. . . . That irreversible element and that it impacts fertility are two big things that I feel really responsible for when making these decisions.

Clinicians sought to manage these concerns by assuring clients that risks do not constitute barriers:

> BAGGA: Trying to be very collaborative and transparent. . . . Hopefully if there are any risks . . . they'll tell me. [Then] we can manage them together.

Regret. Risks for regret are one reason for delaying approval for surgery. However, regret rates are very low—ten out of eleven hundred (Kuiper and Cohen-Kettenis 1998)—and have become a lesser concern for clinicians. What regret means varies: some people detransition; for others it is about social impacts, rather than transition itself. Some clients later conclude it was not the right approach but still accept their decision at the time. Some people are happy with their transition, but their doctors, significant others, or partners think it was a mistake because their quality of life did not improve.

> HARTE: Initially, fear of regret was [very big] due to [being sued at] this clinic. . . . [Other doctors saw it] as problematic, to work with "those kinds of people." And that has certainly changed. . . . Nothing in medicine is a 100 percent guarantee. . . . A regret rate of 1 percent is far better than anything else.

While psychiatrists thought the risk of regret now had limited impact, Bagga saw it as a significant factor:

> BAGGA: It still makes me nervous when I sign off letters for surgery. . . . But I've got faith in the assessments and the process. . . , It's rigorous, it's thorough, and we try and do the best by our patients. . . . I try to be as up front as I can be [with clients about the risk of regret].

The MHPs feel varying levels of responsibility for clients who make decisions they may later regret. Psychologists were more concerned about the impacts of approving surgery, while psychiatrists appear to argue that once they have informed the clients of the risks, it is the client's responsibility. This variation aligns with clients seeing themselves as either patients for whom the clinicians make decisions, or as consumers.

Surgeons' Requirements

For surgeons, little has changed in approval processes over forty years—they want a letter from an experienced MHP saying that people meet *DSM* and *SOC* criteria. They now accept letters from an expanded range of MHPs, and exclusion criteria are looser. More of their clients are younger people who have improved outcomes because of better MHP diagnosis and client preparation, and education by TGD community support groups.

> CEBER: I wouldn't dare to suggest whether somebody should or should not have the operation. . . . Once the [MHPs] have approved somebody, I wasn't going to gatekeep it any further.

> [I'd] refuse the operation for somebody who (a) couldn't understand, or
> (b) was medically unfit. . . . Only two or three in all those years.

Until recently, they would accept referrals only from clinicians associated with the GC—and would send anyone with other referrals to be assessed there. They felt protected from medico-legal risk by the clinic processes:

> CEBER: Having the clinic was very handy initially. . . . I've only had one case related
> to gender reassignment where I was sued and that was due to a medical
> complication.

The surgeons appreciated the good preparation of their gender clients:

> IVES: Some people [ask] "why do you work with TGD people." . . . I say "there's a
> great network." . . . I get a full assessment as to whether surgery is appropri-
> ate. . . . [The clients are] a lot easier to deal with . . . much more well read . . . that
> makes my job ten times easier, that they know all about the operation.

By contrast, with cosmetic genital surgeries for cis-gendered people, the surgeons did few "for comfort" (Ceber), or none (Ives)—mainly owing to medico-legal risks:

> IVES: It's fraught with potential issues. . . . Look at . . . complaints about various
> surgeries, and labiaplasty [and] penile surgery are right up there.

They were very cautious about general cosmetic surgery, suggesting that mental health assessments should be required more widely—as recently introduced in Australia for people under eighteen:

> IVES: In an ideal world, do I think that everyone who's having a cosmetic opera-
> tion should be assessed psychologically? To be honest, yes I think they should. I
> really do.

While most TGD clients come to Ives after seeing experienced GC or private MHPs, he is increasingly approached directly, for both top and bottom surgeries:

> IVES: I say "I'm not a mental health worker . . . so, I can give you information [but]
> as per the *SOC*, you need these reports." . . . Sometimes I get, "oh, I don't need to
> see [MHPs]." It's, "well, actually, you do because I'm not going to do the operation
> without you having that report."

Surgeons did not support an "on-demand" system. While the medical issues are more serious for genital surgery, medico-legal risks are also evident with top surgery:

> IVES: The clinic . . . getting shut down . . . was through a top surgery patient. So, if the *SOC* said you don't need . . . referrals . . . I don't know whether I'd continue doing the work.

> CEBER: The next logical step would be . . . patients just tell the doctor what they want [and] the doctor says yes. . . . You'd end up with all sorts of problem patients. You'd be crazy to take it on.

> HARTE: I put my name to [Bauman 2014 recommending] only one mental health opinion be required for lower surgery. . . . In Australia . . . it would be advisable to be from a psychiatrist [for now]. . . . The surgeons [will] decide what level they want to pitch the quality of referrals.

Given the limited number of TGD surgeons in Australia, it appears unlikely that the situation will soon change from MHP assessment being required for surgery. However, while Ives performed the majority of vaginoplasties in 2017, new surgeons are entering the field, including one who plans to perform phalloplasty.

Discussion

Over forty years, the GC has seen large changes, which have escalated since 2016. However, fundamental aspects of the approval processes for surgery have changed little. Initially run by a small, professionally isolated multidisciplinary group of health practitioners, the GC became dominated by psychiatrists in the 1980s. Now there is a much broader field of professions involved and greater social acceptance for TGD people and the clinicians who provide transition-related services.

The GC's approach has been strongly influenced by global changes in *SOC* and *DSM*, with reduced exclusion criteria, an expanded range of professions approving medical treatments, and movement toward a collaborative model.

Reflecting those global shifts, GC MHPs no longer conceive of gender variance as a psychological disorder with strict exclusion criteria; instead, they see it as a healthy variation. However, other issues may make it advisable to delay medical treatment. Clinicians have genuine concern for their clients; they do not want to deny access to desired treatments, but they want to ensure their clients are aware of risks.

At the interprofessional level, processes to access hormones have recently changed markedly, with clinical psychologists and GPs providing authorization, not only psychiatrists. All GC clinicians now accept that MHP assessment is not always necessary. However, little has changed for the surgeons—they still require a letter from an experienced MHP that confirms that clients meet criteria for the diagnosis after a full mental health assessment.

At the social interaction level of client-clinician relationships, a pivotal experience was being sued by several clients, thus elevating concern regarding risk of regret for many years, and encouraging strict adherence to the *SOC* and *DSM*. This can be seen as MHPs' strengthening gatekeeping after clients did not take responsibility for their decisions, as suggested by Bouman et al. (2014). However, the concerns of clinicians have lessened over time, allowing them to focus less on diagnosis and more on the client's individual journey—which aligns with the principles outlined by Budge and dickey (2017). The shift to clinical psychologist assessments also supports the clients' process of considering their situation and finding the best alternative.

Clinicians have moved to depathologize their approach, but the defining tensions of the clinician-TGD client relationship remain in a balance: risks of regret after treatment versus self-harm without it, and access for clients' desired treatments versus medico-legal risk for the clinician. Dewey and Gesbeck's (2015) argument is partially supported by this evidence—*DSM* and *SOC* changes have not fundamentally shifted the power structures that diagnostic categories maintain over TGD people. However, I would argue that the shifts in MHPs' approaches to diagnosis have lessened, rather than deepened, the pathologization of nonnormative gender expressions.

The changes under way at all levels—in *SOC* and *DSM*, increased public funding, expanded interprofessional collaboration, and improved client-clinician relationships—have resulted in increased access to services, a more trans-affirmative approach in consultations, increased social and therapeutic support, quicker assessment, and a more inclusionary approach to approval of treatments.

To support these developments, future research is needed to explore how clinicians in other settings are changing their approach, and how TGD people view those changes. At the GC, we will seek to take findings to the TGD community for feedback, interview TGD people about their experiences, contribute to state wide TGD health-care system redesign, and contribute to revisions of the *SOC*.

Riki Lane is a research fellow at Monash University in Melbourne, Australia, researching primary health care, and a research/project worker at Monash Health's Gender Clinic. Doctoral and subsequent work has investigated the social and political implications of the "brain-sex" theory of trans, and the shifting paradigms in trans and gender-diverse health care.

Notes

1.   I use *trans and gender diverse* (TGD) for people who live in a social gender different from their sex assigned at birth, including those with a nonbinary gender, and *gender variance* more generally for variation from a female/male dichotomy. This language is contested and constantly changing. *TGD* is widely used by Australian community organizations such as Transgender Victoria. Due to community consultation while this article has been in process, the Gender Clinic is now using *trans, gender diverse, and nonbinary* (TGDNB).

2.   The Monash Health Gender Clinic changed its name from the Monash Health Gender Dysphoria Clinic in 2017, acting on advice from the recently established Consumer Advisory Panel.

References

APA (American Psychiatric Association). 2013. *Diagnostic and Statistical Manual of Mental Disorders*. 5th ed. Arlington, VA: American Psychiatric Association.

Bouman, W. P., et al. 2014. "Yes and Yes Again: Are Standards of Care Which Require Two Referrals for Genital Reconstructive Surgery Ethical?" *Sexual and Relationship Therapy* 29, no. 4: 377–89. doi.org/10.1080/14681994.2014.954993.

Budge, Stephanie L., and lore m. dickey. 2017. "Barriers, Challenges, and Decision-Making in the Letter Writing Process for Gender Transition." *Psychiatric Clinics of North America* 40, no. 1: 65–78. doi.org/10.1016/j.psc.2016.10.001.

Coleman, Eli, et al. 2012. "Standards of Care for the Health of Transsexual, Transgender, and Gender-Nonconforming People, Version Seven." *International Journal of Transgenderism* 13, no. 4: 165–232.

Corrigan, Patrick W. 2005. *On the Stigma of Mental Illness: Practical Strategies for Research and Social Change*. Washington, DC: American Psychological Association.

De Cuypere, Griet, and Sam Winter. 2016. "A Gender Incongruence Diagnosis: Where to Go?" *Lancet Psychiatry* 3, no. 9: 796–97.

Deutsch, Madeline B. 2012. "Use of the Informed Consent Model in the Provision of Cross-Sex Hormone Therapy: A Survey of the Practices of Selected Clinics." *International Journal of Transgenderism* 13, no. 3: 140–46. doi.org/10.1080/15532739.2011.675233.

Dewey, Jodie M., and Melissa M. Gesbeck. 2015. "(Dys) Functional Diagnosing: Mental Health Diagnosis, Medicalization, and the Making of Transgender Patients." *Humanity and Society* 41, no. 1: 37–72. doi.org/10.1177/0160597615604651.

Drescher, Jack, Peggy T. Cohen-Kettenis, and Geoffrey M. Reed. 2016. "Gender Incongruence of Childhood in the ICD-11: Controversies, Proposal, and Rationale." *Lancet Psychiatry* 3, no. 3: 297–304. doi.org/10.1016/S2215-0366(15)00586-6.

Epstein, Steven. 1996. *Impure Science: AIDS, Activism, and the Politics of Knowledge, Medicine, and Society*. Berkeley: University of California Press.

Fraser, Lin, and Gail Knudson. 2017. "Past and Future Challenges Associated with Standards of Care for Gender Transitioning Clients." *Psychiatric Clinics of North America* 40, no. 1: 15–27. doi.org/10.1016/j.psc.2016.10.012.

HBIGDA (Harry Benjamin International Gender Dysphonia Association). 1985. "Standards of Care: The Hormonal and Surgical Sex Reassignment of Gender Dysphoric Persons. Harry Benjamin International Gender Dysphonia Association." *Archives of Sexual Behavior* 14, no. 1: 79–90.

Jaarsma, Pier, and Stellan Welin. 2012. "Autism as a Natural Human Variation: Reflections on the Claims of the Neurodiversity Movement." *Health Care Analysis* 20, no. 1: 20–30. doi.org/10.1007/s10728-011-0169-9.

Jutel, Annemarie, and Sarah Nettleton. 2011. "Towards a Sociology of Diagnosis: Reflections and Opportunities." *Social Science and Medicine* 73, no. 6: 793–800.

Kirk, Sheila, and Claudette Kulkarni. 2006. "The Whole Person: A Paradigm for Integrating the Mental and Physical Health of Trans Clients." In *The Handbook of Lesbian, Gay, Bisexual, and Transgender Public Health: A Practitioner's Guide to Service*, edited by Michael D. Shankle, 145–74. New York: Haworth Reference.

Kuiper, A. J., and P. T. Cohen-Kettenis. 1998. "Gender Role Reversal among Postoperative Transsexuals." *International Journal of Transgenderism* 2, no. 3.

Lane, Riki. 2012. "Paradigm and Power Shifts in the Gender Clinic." In *Technologies of Sexuality, Identity, and Sexual Health*, edited by Lenore Manderson, 205–30. Abingdon, UK: Routledge.

Lev, Arlene Istar. 2004. *Transgender Emergence: Therapeutic Guidelines for Working with Gender-Variant People and Their Families*. Haworth Marriage and the Family. New York: Haworth Clinical Practice.

———. 2013. "Gender Dysphoria: Two Steps Forward, One Step Back." *Clinical Social Work Journal* 41, no. 3: 288–96. doi.org/10.1007/s10615-013-0447-0.

Robles, Rebeca, et al. 2016. "Removing Transgender Identity from the Classification of Mental Disorders: A Mexican Field Study for ICD-11." *Lancet Psychiatry* 3, no. 9: 850–59. doi.org/10.1016/S2215-0366(16)30165-1.

Rogers, Anne, and David Pilgrim. 2005. *A Sociology of Mental Health and Illness*. 3rd ed. Maidenhead, UK: Open University Press.

Selvaggi, Gennaro, and Simona Giordano. 2014. "The Role of Mental Health Professionals in Gender Reassignment Surgeries: Unjust Discrimination or Responsible Care?" *Aesthetic Plastic Surgery* 38, no. 6: 1177–83. doi.org/10.1007/s00266-014-0409-0.

Smith, Elizabeth, et al. 2014. *From Blues to Rainbows: The Mental Health and Well-Being of Gender Diverse and Transgender Young People in Australia*. Bundoora, Australia: La Trobe University.

Willis, Evan. 1983. *Medical Dominance: The Division of Labour in Australian Health Care*. Studies in Society. Sydney: George Allen and Unwin.

Medical Transition without Social Transition

Expanding Options for Privately Gendered Bodies

KATHERINE RACHLIN

Abstract People who want gender-affirming surgery without a change in social role represent a range of unique perspectives and use a range of self-descriptive terms, including *transgender, transsexual, genderqueer, gender nonconforming, TGNC, nonbinary*, and *cross-dresser*. They may seek surgery to reduce gender dysphoria or to enhance gender euphoria. Professional literature and medical protocols such as the World Professional Association for Transgender Health's (WPATH) *Standards of Care*, version 7 (*SOC*-7), have been developed to reflect the needs of people who want to change their social role as well as their body. Medical protocols including *SOC*-7 recommend a period of "real-life experience" as a criterion for some surgeries, which is not appropriate for people who want medical without social transition, who may want a private expression of gender, and who are at high risk for self-treatment and self-injury. This article describes the many factors that may affect transition and surgical choices. A composite case example is presented to illustrate how surgery without social transition might enhance the life of a female-identified person who lives socially as a man. Medical and mental health providers do provide treatment for people who want medical transition without social transition, but the practice has yet to be well documented.
Keywords transgender, nonbinary, gender-affirming surgery, Standards of Care, real-life experience

This article addresses the needs of people who want gender-affirming surgery without a change in social role. These individuals may identify as transgender, transsexual, gender nonconforming, or nonbinary, but unlike some people who claim these identities, this group is committed to a social gender presentation consistent with their birth-assigned gender. Nonsocially transitioning individuals have a strong desire to change the gendered characteristics of their body for personal affirmation and comfort. Some may ideally want full gender transition, but for a range of reasons, discussed below, they may opt to change their body without changing their public presentation or gender role.

TSQ: Transgender Studies Quarterly ★ Volume 5, Number 2 ★ May 2018 **228**
DOI 10.1215/23289252-4348660   © 2018 Duke University Press

For some people, physical without social change represents a compromise, and for others it is their optimal choice. Some individuals are gender dysphoric, experiencing distress surrounding their assigned gender and gendered body. Others do not experience dysphoria but do experience gender euphoria—exceptionally good feelings from a gender expression or from the experience of a gendered body different from that of their birth-assigned gender.[1] Many people use medical transition to serve their desire for full expression of gender in the social realm. For others, a gendered body is a private pleasure. Surgery allows these individuals to privately experience joy when they come home in the evening and put gender-affirming clothing on a body that feels authentic. They feel good when they see their body in the mirror after a shower, experience their body intact through the night and under their clothes through the day. Like anyone else, they may share their body with a partner, or they may not.

Transition is the term used to refer to the process of changing from one gender presentation to another. Medical transition may involve the use of hormones or surgery to make one more comfortable with one's gendered body. Social transition involves making changes in relation to other people in order to interact with others in the world in one's affirmed gender role and gender expression. Social transition may encompass family, work, friends, public persona, legal status, and changes in documentation. In a binary paradigm, an individual would commonly transition from one gender (female or male) to another gender (female or male). Broader definitions of transition have evolved alongside conceptions of gender identity. Widely used medical protocols now recognize that individuals may transition from one gender presentation to another, but the genders are not necessarily male or female. This change is reflected in the American Psychiatric Association's *Diagnostic and Statistical Manual*, fifth edition (APA 2013), and the World Professional Association for Transgender Health's (WPATH) *Standards of Care for the Health of Transsexual, Transgender, and Gender Nonconforming People*, version 7 (WPATH 2011).

Gender is a social phenomenon that exists between and among people. When individuals express differently in private than in public, it breaks a social contract that says that gender is readable, comprehensible, and shared. The privately gendered body also betrays the traditional narrative that an individual seeking surgery needs an appropriate body through which to express themselves socially in their affirmed gender. By wanting only a private experience of a surgically altered body, the nontransitioning person removes from the equation an argument that has been essential to those who advocate for access to surgery. Yet, even while appearing gender normative, they challenge established gender norms. They may be seen as closeted, compromised, or privileged; they may decline to be public or political, yet they are in fact taking major risks in securing a nonbinary, nonconforming body on their own terms. Despite community disquiet about passing privilege, people who transition medically but not socially challenge conventions. Like all people who undergo gender-affirming surgery, they knowingly make themselves vulnerable to unwanted exposure. Though they may maintain privacy through most of their lives, they share with all transgender people the likelihood that there will come a time when they may be forced to surrender privacy because of hospitalization or end-of-life events.

Because of the nonpublic nature of this expression, nonsocially transitioning people are often unrecognized in the transgender community, the professional literature, and medical protocols that have been developed in response to the needs of people who want to change their social role as well as their body. Among individuals who request gender-affirming surgery, those who want medical without social transition are the least visible, and their voices are rarely heard or represented. Individuals who receive gender-affirming medical treatment without social transition are often known to their medical and mental health providers, but they continue to be elusive in the research literature. In other words, some health-care providers *do* provide services for nonsocially transitioning individuals, yet official diagnostic and medical protocols reflect the expectation that individuals seeking surgery will enact a change in social role as well (APA 2013; Bockting and Goldberg 2006; Bouman et al. 2014; Colebunders, De Cuypere, and Monstrey 2015; Coleman et al. 2012; Hembree et al. 2017).

The transgender community and transgender rights movement in the United States have successfully advocated on behalf of people who pursue some form of social transition without medical transition (National Center for Transgender Equality 2018; Iowa Civil Rights Commission 2016; Spade 2003; Transgender Legal Defense and Education Fund 2018). In some locations, advances in social policy have allowed individuals to change legal documents to match their identity regardless of their physical or surgical status (for example, a transgender woman whose legal identity documents reflect her identity as a woman regardless of whether she has undergone gender-affirming surgery) (van Anders, Caverly, and Johns 2014). There has also been progress toward public accommodation and gender-affirming medical care, including surgery, for individuals who express nonbinary and gender-nonconforming identities (Segal 2016), but there remains a lack of advocacy on behalf of people who want gender-affirming surgery for personal comfort without any external transition or visible gender nonconformity.

Why has this group been neglected in the midst of the LGBTQ and TGGNC movements in which inclusivity has been a central value? The answer lies in the heart of the experience of wanting medical without social transition: the desire for privacy and a private expression of gender. A person's desire for privacy, and even secrecy, can challenge the values of trans-positive advocates and allies.

Visibility politics and the imperative to be out may exclude or obscure nonsocially transitioning individuals. They are a diverse group, and their most comfortable gender expression may not require a public expression. In essence, there is no "out" to move toward if they are already living in their preferred social role. They often articulate the feeling that there is nothing to be gained by discussing this desire with other people or by being public about their private desire. And, for some, privacy is part of the pleasure.

In light of this tendency toward private expression, it is no surprise that nonsocially transitioning individuals are often isolated. Some do not feel a need for connection, but many do want to know that they are not alone. They are curious about how others have managed this experience. Despite the desire for connection, they may avoid community because they do not identify as transgender or are protective of their gender-normative social status and do not want to risk disclosure of themselves or for their family. Even if they go to community forums, they may have difficulty finding individuals like themselves because their true peers are not out as transgender, and after fighting for the right to openly express themselves, transgender community members may not be interested in supporting those who choose not to do so. The idea of supporting people who want a more private affirmation without public expression may go against the spirit of the trans support forums that value the free social expression of gender identity. There is also a tendency for others to see this as "a phase" on the road to a more fully realized gender transition. This presumption discounts the experience of the individual in the moment and does not allow for the possibility that this may be a legitimate and long-term position.

It is often assumed that the drive to resolve a gender-incongruent body will be matched with the drive to resolve a gender-incongruent social life and that these things coexist equally within an individual, yet there are a range of people who believe it is in their best interest to change their bodies, but not their social roles. In my experience, people who request medical without social transition include the following:

- transgender people who want to take change one step at a time with hope that full transition with all its disruption and expense may not be necessary,
- individuals who strongly identify with their assigned social role but who are not comfortable with the gendered characteristics of their body,
- people who have strong desires to change the gendered characteristics of their body while knowing that the highest quality of life is to be had in their assigned gender role,
- people who alternate gender expressions but live primarily in their assigned gender,

- people who find that there is no acceptable social role that reflects their true gender identity, so that while satisfying physical changes are possible, social expression is limited. This may be the case for nonbinary individuals who want physical alterations to create bodies that fully express nonbinary identities. Without a sanctioned social role for nonbinary people, social expression can be complicated. Some nonbinary people will say that they already have full social expression of their gender, while others may say that the lack of an established social role makes full social expression unattainable (for example, the inability to have official documents that indicate nonbinary and the difficulty of being accurately perceived by other people as nonbinary). Though social expression may be difficult, for some, personal goals for nonbinary expression of the body may be fully realized through hormones and/or surgery, and
- eunuch-identified people who require surgery for comfort with their gender identity and gendered body but who have no visible social role in Western culture to transition toward.[2]

Many people who identify as transgender seek a compromise between their wish for full gender transition and practical limitations. Below are some limitations that might apply to either medical or social transition:

- Career concerns: while some people transition on the job, others are sure to lose their source of income, and many expect that it will be difficult to find employment posttransition.
- Health: health problems may prohibit undergoing medical treatments necessary for transition.
- Culture and social ostracism: some people will lose essential social support.
- Religion: religious beliefs that prohibit gender expression may not be reconcilable.
- Low tolerance for risk: transition requires that people risk things that they value. A person may be unwilling to risk losing their partner, family, or community.
- Fragility: transition is extremely difficult, and not everyone has sufficient energy and resiliency.
- Primary caretaker for others: transition may compromise the ability to carry on in this role.
- Dependent on others: transition may fracture relationships necessary for survival.
- Documentation and institutional issues: in some circumstances, one cannot change one's official name and/or gender on official identity documents such as passports, driver's license, and so forth. Gender transition may lead one to

be barred from marrying or adopting children and make one vulnerable to discrimination in housing and employment.

- Unachievable desires: some individuals determine that they could never achieve their desired physical or social outcome because of the limitations of the social environment and current medical interventions. No medical interventions can completely undo the results of previous puberty, make one younger, or provide all the features of a natal body (such as reproductive capacity). They anticipate that they will not be satisfied with their appearance or with their social, professional, or family life if they go through a medical and social transition.

- Self-sacrifice for loved ones: depending on a person's culture and values, they may prioritize the needs of the group or the family over the needs of the individual. For this, and many other reasons, people make sacrifices for the people they love. Denying or delaying social gender transition can be one such sacrifice.

- Social hostilities: transition may make one vulnerable to increased social stigma, prejudice, and violence. This is especially true in cultures in which gender variance is a crime.

The above lists demonstrate that there are many factors that have nothing to do with gender identity that affect transition choices. People who face these complicated choices and do not go through social transition, or who postpone transition, may still request surgery. Fortunately, because of the long history of patient satisfaction achieved with gender-affirming medical care, gender specialists are often comfortable tailoring treatment to exceptional cases with the knowledge that such treatment is potentially life enhancing (Carroll 1999; Ehrbar and Gorton 2011; Murad et al. 2010; Gijs and Brewaeys 2007; Pfäfflin and Junge 1998).

As a psychologist and gender specialist in private practice for more than twenty years, I have had as part of my job helping people explore their feelings and fears and to overcome obstacles in their lives. When a member of a family goes through a gender transition, I work with that family to support everyone involved. One of the most common situations I encounter in my work is male-assigned individuals who live as husbands and fathers while wishing they could express themselves as women. Individuals who find themselves in this situation may move in a number of different directions, including toward a full social gender transition. For those of us who are aware of that trajectory, it might seem that a female-identified person living in a male role is a transgender woman simply in need of liberation. But that would be too simplistic and offer too limited a range of options to suit the diversity of individuals who have such experience. Some of the people in this group do not want to socially transition. Their goal is to have a body that is syntonic with the feminine aspects of their identity while continuing to live in the male role.[3] They may have appeared to others as gender normative and gender conforming all of their lives. Or they may have early life stories of childhood female identification and feminine expression met with parental disapproval, bullying by other children, early and ongoing clandestine cross-dressing, and some sporadic use of hormones and/or past movement toward transition. Many people with that life experience come to gender-oriented psychotherapy to explore the possibilities and gain support for gender transition. But this nonsocially transitioning group comes to psychotherapy with the goal of satisfying their desire for a feminine body while maintaining their male social role. If they are gender dysphoric,[4] they want to manage dysphoric feelings without transitioning, and they may hold onto that goal even after long periods of gender-affirming therapy.

It is important to distinguish between advocacy on behalf of nonsocially transitioning individuals and reparative therapy. Reparative therapy seeks to curb an individual's natural inclinations. Trans-positive gender-affirming care supports the individual in their own goals for gender expression and does so with the understanding that those goals can change over time and that all gender identities and forms of expression are equally valid (Coleman et al. 2012; De Cuypere, Knudson, and Bockting 2010; Ehrensaft 2016; Lev 2004; Singh and dickey 2017).

Below is a composite story based on the many people I have worked with over the years who have sought a supportive therapeutic environment in which to share their inner self and to explore options for self-expression. It illustrates a common experience of individuals who request surgery without engaging in a social transition. I call this individual Michael, her male name, though I will use feminine pronouns to reflect her internal identity. This reflects the way that Michael lives. Because she views my office as an extension of her private life, she wants me to recognize and know her this way. For many people like Michael, I am the only person with whom they share their private name. In this article, I refer to her as Michael because I am advocating for her right to privacy, and Michael is the way she is known in the public sphere. All of my clients have been to my website, which explicitly states that I am supportive of all gender expressions, including individuals who choose not to transition. I frequently receive calls from people saying that the reason they called me is that I specifically mentioned "non-transitioning individuals."

Michael is a forty-one-year-old Irish American who lives as a man and has a lifelong private female identity. She is a devout Catholic and is the director of the parochial school of her family church where four generations of her family currently attend. She is a conservative and traditional person, politically, religiously, and socially. She has been married for twelve years, and she and her wife have five children between the ages of three and eleven.

Michael first came to therapy six years ago because she was feeling internal pressure to change her body and express herself as a woman, which was distracting her from her work and family. Despite these feelings, she did not want to trade her current male role and social status for a life as a woman. She had obtained feminizing hormones on the Internet and had been self-medicating for two years. After coming to therapy, she began seeing a medical doctor who has overseen her care on a low dose of hormones for approximately four years. This dosage has provided physical changes that soothe her need to be feminine but are not so great that they cannot be hidden under clothing. She feels that the physical changes have partially freed her from her male body by creating a softer and more feminine form.

So far, this is a fairly standard scenario in my practice. Some people in Michael's position go on to explore gender options, decide to transition, and work hard to help their families adjust to the change. Some stay in their marriages and some do not. Michael's dysphoria is balanced by her concern for her family and attachment to her lifestyle. If that balance changes, she may feel compelled to transition or have more public expression. But for now, that is not what she wants. It is not what she most needs. Michael enjoys her present career, family life, and social life, and she does not envision that the life she could realistically attain as a woman would be a better option. Though the situation is not perfect, this compromise is the best possible path she can see for herself at this time. She finds freedom in being able to make decisions that support her values as well as her need for feminization.

Before getting married, Michael told her wife, Sheri, that internally she was a woman but had every intention of keeping this desire private. Sheri said that she wanted to marry a man and that if Michael could not promise to remain a man, then they should not get married. Michael made that promise.[5] Over the years, she has continued to experience desire for a female body and has occasionally talked to Sheri about this desire. According to Michael, Sheri did not like to talk about this and remained quiet when the subject came up. She was aware when Michael began psychotherapy but declined multiple invitations to participate, to engage in couples therapy, or to get therapy for herself. When Michael decided to go on hormones, she told Sheri that it was for private comfort. Sheri initially resisted but was able to adjust over time, especially because she saw that there was no disruption to their social, professional, or family lives. As Michael's body became more feminine, Sheri became less attracted to her. The two were affectionate but had not been sexual since the birth of their last child. When Michael recently told Sheri that she was thinking of having vaginoplasty, Sheri was very sad but not surprised. Despite her sadness, Sheri wants to go to surgery with Michael, and they have an appointment to see a surgeon together in the coming months.

While most of the clinical practitioners I know are familiar with the administration of hormones to support people living in their assigned gender, a smaller number of practitioners have experience providing surgical interventions for this group. Hormones are often regarded as more reversible than surgery, so the bar to access is lower. Also, the path to access surgery usually involves more medical resources, and the procedure must be justified through diagnostic codes that often affect rental of surgical suites/operating rooms as well as the services of the anesthesiologist, surgeon(s), nursing and surgical support staff, and hospital inpatient services. Even when medical providers want to provide services to nonsocially transitioning people, they may be held back by hospital policies or insurance company guidelines such as the 2017 insurance plan for Empire Blue Cross Blue Shield Policy, which states:

> For individuals undergoing sex reassignment surgery . . . it is considered **medically necessary** when *all* of the following criteria are met: . . . The individual has been diagnosed with gender dysphoria, and exhibits all of the following: 1. The desire to live and be accepted as a member of the opposite sex, usually accompanied by the wish to make his or her body as congruent as possible with the preferred sex through surgery and hormone treatment; 2. Documentation that the individual has completed a minimum of 12 months of successful continuous full time real-life experience in their new gender, across a wide range of life experiences and events that may occur throughout the year (for example, family events, holidays, vacations, season-specific work or school experiences). This includes coming out to partners, family, friends, and community members (for example, at school, work, and other settings). (Empire Blue Cross Blue Shield 2017)

Individuals who do not fulfill these requirements can be denied coverage or reimbursement for surgical expenses (Aetna 2017; Empire Blue Cross Blue Shield 2017). The usual definition of the "real-life experience" is constructed so that a person lives before surgery as one will live after surgery. A case can be made that for individuals who have no intention of ever living in a gender other than the one assigned at birth, living in their assigned gender and expressing their identity privately is "real-life experience." The person will often report decades of stable and enduring outward-but-private expression, such as wearing gender-affirming undergarments or night clothes, with or without the use of hormones. If "real-life experience" is a criterion for surgery, then it should be expanded to include such partial or site-specific expression.

Historically, support for individually tailored medical transition goes back to Harry Benjamin's 1966 book, *The Transsexual Phenomenon*, in which he identified a continuum of identity and desire for medical intervention, with some individuals utilizing cross-gender hormones while living in their assigned gender. At the 1981 symposium of the Harry Benjamin International Gender Dysphoria Association conference in Jerusalem, Drs. Christine Wheeler and Leah Schaefer presented a paper titled "The Nonsurgical True Transsexual (Benjamin's Category IV): A Theoretical Rationale" (1984). In this paper they argued that some transsexual women will not have genital surgery for a variety of reasons and that they live well as women without such surgery. This paper challenged the assumption that all transsexual people wanted and needed genital surgery, thus disconnecting the presumed association between medical and social transition. More than a decade later, the 1998 version of the Harry Benjamin International Gender Dysphoria Association's (now WPATH) *Standards of Care* described the standard transition trajectory as "a triadic therapeutic sequence (real life experience [a form of social transition], hormones, and surgery)" (Levin et al. 1998). A 1999 paper that challenged that assumption looked at how transgender men make decisions regarding genital surgery. The study found that the respondents had a range of goals for surgery even though they all identified as men and the majority were living as men. A man might choose metoidioplasty, phalloplasty, or no surgery; but one could not predict his decision based solely on his gender identity (Rachlin 1999). This research has been used to advocate for the rights of transmasculine people to be treated as men regardless of their surgical status.[6] Both papers attempted to challenge the traditional assumptions linking social transition and surgical transition. This article attempts to disconnect the same link, but rather than advocating for the social without the surgical, it advocates for the surgical without the social. This seems to me to be a natural and reasonable evolution of thought, as treatment protocols are constantly evolving to reflect the needs of trans and gender-nonconforming people (Meyer et al. 2001; Coleman et al. 2012).

Today virtually all of the major texts in transgender health are highly supportive of individualized care for transgender and gender-nonconforming individuals (Beek et. al. 2015; Colebunders, De Cuypere, and Monstrey 2015; Bockting and Coleman 1992; Bockting and Goldberg 2006; Ettner, Monstrey, and Coleman 2016; Lev 2004; Singh and dickey 2017; Krieger 2017), and a number of authors have published papers that assert the need for gender-affirming medical care for people who do not fit the GID/GD/transsexual diagnosis (Hage and Karim 2000; Johnson and Wassersug 2010; Rachlin, Dhejne, and Brown 2010; Vale et al. 2010). The field of transgender health is evolving to address the needs of nonbinary and gender-nonconforming individuals, but there has been no such organized effort to meet the needs of those who seek medical without social transition while living in their affirmed binary gender.

Griet De Cuypere, Gail Knudson, and Walter Bockting (2010) and Peggy Cohen-Kettenis and Friedemann Pfäfflin (2010) reviewed the *Diagnostic and Statistical Manual of Mental Disorders* (*DSM*-IV-TR; APA 2000) diagnostic criteria for gender identity disorder and made recommendations for the then upcoming *DSM*-5 (APA 2013). Both groups of authors recommended criteria that would "capture the spectrum of gender variance phenomena" and facilitate appropriate flexible treatment for a diverse population. The *DSM*-5 has, in fact, addressed the need for more flexible treatment criteria for transgender and nonconforming individuals. However, that explicit support is more focused on gender expression and does not address desire for medical intervention while continuing to live in one's assigned role. The quote below, from the *DSM*-5, illustrates the expectation that transgender individuals will desire a social role outside their assigned gender.

> They feel uncomfortable being regarded by others, or functioning in society, as members of their assigned gender. Some adults may have a strong desire to be of a different gender and treated as such, and they may have an inner certainty to feel and respond as the experienced gender without seeking medical treatment to alter body characteristics. They may find other ways to resolve the incongruence between experienced/expressed and assigned gender by partially living in the desired role or by adopting a gender role neither conventionally male nor conventionally female. (APA 2013: 454)

Support for gender diversity is also seen in WPATH's *SOC*-7 (Coleman et al. 2012). The *SOC*, which encourages practitioners to flexibly tailor treatment to individual needs, states clearly and repeatedly that not all transgender people want or need hormones or surgery and very specifically addresses the needs of gender-nonconforming individuals. *SOC*-7 has this to say in support of medical without social transition: "Hormone therapy must be individualized based on a patient's goals, the risk/benefit ratio of medications, the presence of other medical conditions, and consideration of social and economic issues. Hormone therapy can provide significant comfort to patients who do not wish to make a social gender role transition or undergo surgery, or who are unable to do so" (Coleman et al. 2012). Britt Colebunders, Griet De Cuypere, and Stan Monstrey (2015) reviewed the seventh version of the *SOC* and gave their recommendations for changes to be included in *SOC*-8. They called for the standards to do an even better job in addressing gender diversity; however, the authors did not articulate support for access to surgery for people who are not gender dysphoric, nor did they discuss access to medical without social transition.

Randall D. Ehrbar and R. Nicholas Gorton noted in their paper on provider treatment models (2011: 204), "Of the treatment combinations available to patients including social transition, hormones, genital surgery, and non-genital surgery, the single combination that is precluded by the *SOC* is genital surgery without social transition." And this continues in version 7. This recommendation rests on two ideas: that physical transition is ultimately in the service of social transition, and that social transition is less invasive and more reversible than physical interventions. While this is true for many people, coming out is not a neutral act. Claiming a transgender identity and undergoing a social gender change in the world of family and work is also a huge and irreversible undertaking that may result in loss of friends, family, and career. Social transition, too, contains considerable risk.

Ehrbar and Gorton explore the nature and flexibility of individual providers and clinics who treat transgender individuals. "Provider-level customization of the SOC is common, but rarely is made explicit or articulated to clients," they write (2011: 209). "Providers who prefer social transition preceding physical interventions may perceive social transition as more reversible. Providers who are comfortable beginning with physical transition may focus more on the irreversible aspects of social transition such as disclosure to family. The risk of an intervention depends not only on the specific intervention but on the context of a client's life" (200).

In many fields of medicine, harm reduction guides treatment decisions, and in transgender medicine it is a major reason that providers "break the rules." Under most contemporary medical systems, a person must meet diagnostic criteria to receive treatment (for any situation, not only gender-affirming care). However, an exception may be made if it can be shown that withholding treatment will put the patient at great risk. It is widely acknowledged that gender-nonconforming individuals who do not fit traditional paradigms may self-medicate by accessing hormones on the Internet; they may get the surgery they want by telling therapists or doctors what they think the gatekeepers want to hear, and in some cases, they may perform risky self-surgery (Brown 2010). Male-to-eunuch identified individuals are one of the groups which raise the question of how to provide surgical interventions for people who would benefit from surgical procedures but who lack the social experience that has been used to justify gender-affirming surgeries for others (Ehrbar 2011; Johnson and Irwig 2014; Vale et al. 2010).

I approached Dr. Loren S. Schechter, MD, FACS, director of the Center for Gender Confirmation Surgery at Louis A. Weiss Memorial Hospital, Chicago, to ask about his work with transgender individuals who want surgery without social transition. He identified both orchiectomy alone and also vaginoplasty as options for individuals who were not intent on full social transition, as "they tend to be professional people who have work-related challenges about transitioning socially. They may be trying to stay married and don't want their kids to know. We see a spectrum of where people are at and a lot of practical matters come into play—how they decide to do it and when they decide to do it. There are unique circumstances for every situation" (Schechter, pers. comm., March 1, 2017).This brief comment is an illustration of the applied flexibility in gender-affirming surgical practice that rarely appears in scholarly papers or textbooks. It is a glimpse into the practice of how experienced trans-sensitive surgeons use the *Standards of Care* flexibly to tailor treatment to individual needs.

How do current medical treatment protocols serve the needs of people like Michael? She fulfills all the *DSM*-5 diagnostic criteria for gender dysphoria, and by most definitions, she would be considered transgender because her gender assigned at birth does not reflect the totality of her gender identity, but she is not seeking the social transition often expected of people who seek gender-affirming surgery. One can see why it would be unreasonable to require that Michael socially express herself as a woman to obtain surgery. This raises two questions: Why would medical protocols require that any transgender woman or male-assigned person on the feminine spectrum come out at work and risk losing her job if she prefers to be fulfilled by expressing herself as a woman in her private life? Why would she be required to take hormone therapy, which will make her appear more feminine to the rest of the world, if what she really wants is the private experience of vaginoplasty and to maintain her life without undue disruption?

As discussed above, clinical protocols often recommend a period of "real-life experience" prior to gender-affirming surgery, but I challenge this recommendation with a focus on people for whom a social "real-life experience" would be completely inappropriate and irrelevant. Rather than approach the private desire for female embodiment from a sexological perspective, I address it from a pragmatic perspective. My starting point is that of respect for the individual who knows themselves and knows what they want. I am advocating for increased possibilities for self-determination. I would prefer not to put diagnostic labels on the nonsocially transitioning individuals who are the subject of this article, though many will fulfill some or all of the criteria for a *DSM*-5 diagnosis of gender dysphoria, other specified gender dysphoria, or unspecified gender dysphoria (APA 2013), or the ICD-10 criteria for a diagnosis of transsexualism. It is my contention that as a group they are best seen as complex individuals who are generally thoughtful and capable of making practical decisions. My recommendation is that professionals document the care already being provided to these individuals so that medical providers will feel confident in giving gender-affirming care to those who want medical without social transition. Gains made here will also support the ongoing efforts of gender-nonconforming, nonbinary, and eunuch-identified individuals who also need access to surgery. Treatment protocols that reflect the needs of these populations would define *real-life experience* as "living before surgery the way one expects to live after surgery." Patient-sensitive practice would shift to an informed consent model focused on the person's ability to consent to surgery with a standard assessment of whether they understand the risks and complications of the procedure. The transgender umbrella is so broad that all who request gender-affirming medical care can be included within it. Diagnosis, while necessary for treatment in the current medical system, may be less important than assessment of decision-making skills, and informed consent. This model has long been used to access hormones in community-based health centers in the United States and can become the path to access surgery as well.

If health-care providers want to help individuals to reduce dysphoria and increase comfort, they must take into account the individual's culture, environment, resources, and personality, as well as their gender identity and desires. A treatment strategy that is minimally disruptive respects the need for privacy, for inclusion in one's community of origin, and sometimes the need to express as one truly wishes. People should not have to sacrifice their worldview, community, family, or faith to receive treatment.

Katherine Rachlin, PhD, is a clinical psychologist and gender specialist. She has served on the APA's Taskforce on Gender Identity, Gender Variance, and Intersex Conditions, on the board of directors of FTM International, and, from 2013 to the present, on the board of directors of WPATH. Her published articles address such topics as the flexible use of the Standards of Care and factors influencing trans surgery decisions.

Notes

1.   *Gender euphoria* is not an official diagnostic term, as is *gender dysphoria*. The term reflects the recognition that transgender individuals do not necessarily come from a place of discomfort or suffering but may be self-actualizing from and toward a positive experience. Gender euphoria is a common motivation for moving into an affirmed gender, gender role, expression, or private embodiment. It is possible to feel both gender dysphoria and gender euphoria at different times or regarding different aspects of experience. For example, a person may feel dysphoria/sadness and discomfort regarding gendered aspects of their body and gender euphoria when they experience gender affirmation alone or with others.

2.   Kayla Vale et al. (2010) have published "The Development of Standards of Care for Individuals with a Male-to-Eunuch Gender Identity Disorder" to address the needs of this population. For a specifically Chinese perspective on eunuchs, see Chaing 2012.

3.   A period of private exploration and development is quite common for people who later become much more public and want social engagement and transition. However, not

everyone will follow that path. It is respectful to accept the individual's own statement regarding their identity and desire, while keeping all options open for the future.

4. Oxford Living Dictionaries defines *dysphoria* as "a state of unease or dissatisfaction" and "the opposite of euphoria" (accessed July 22, 2017, en.oxforddictionaries.com/definition /dysphoria). The essence of the *DSM*-5 diagnostic category "gender dysphoria" is a discomfort with one's assigned gender and a wish to be of the "opposite or some other gender" (APA 2000).

5. Such promises made under duress are not fair or reasonable. Many people who promise to suppress their affirmed gender reach a time in life when they feel compelled to express their true self. Thus after years of struggle, the promise is broken.

6. Historically, there has been an asymmetry between trans men and women regarding the centrality of surgical transition. I believe that this discrepancy is multidimensional, with technological, political, and cultural factors playing varying roles. A full discussion of this is beyond the scope of this article and the reader is referred to Meyerowitz 2004.

References

Aetna. 2017. "Gender Reassignment Surgery." www.aetna.com/cpb/medical/data/600_699/0615 .html (accessed July 23, 2017).

APA (American Psychiatric Association). 2000. *Diagnostic and Statistical Manual of Mental Disorders*. 4th ed., text rev. Arlington, VA: American Psychiatric Association.

———. 2013. *Diagnostic and Statistical Manual of Mental Disorders*. 5th ed. Arlington, VA: American Psychiatric Association.

Beek, Titia F., Baudewijntje P. C. Kreukels, Peggy T. Cohen-Kettenis, and Thomas Steensma. 2015. "Partial Treatment Requests and Underlying Motives of Applicants for Gender Affirming Interventions." *Journal of Sexual Medicine* 12, no. 11: 2201–5.

Benjamin, Harry. 1966. *The Transsexual Phenomenon*. New York: Julian.

Bockting, Walter O., and Eli Coleman. 1992. "A Comprehensive Approach to the Treatment of Gender Dysphoria." In *Gender Dysphoria: Interdisciplinary Approaches in Clinical Management*, edited by Walter O. Bockting and Eli Coleman, 131–55. Binghamton, NY: Haworth.

Bockting, Walter O., and Joshua M. Goldberg. 2006. *Guidelines for Transgender Care*. Binghamton, NY: Haworth Medical.

Bouman, Walter P., et al. 2014. "Yes and Yes Again: Are Standards of Care Which Require Two Referrals for Genital Reconstructive Surgery Ethical?" *Sexual and Relationship Therapy* 29, no. 4: 377–89. doi.org/10.1080/14681994.2014.954993.

Brown, George R. 2010. "Autocastration and Autopenectomy as Surgical Self-Treatment in Incarcerated Persons with Gender Identity Disorder." *International Journal of Transgenderism* 12, no. 1: 31–39.

Carroll, Richard. 1999. "Outcomes of Treatment for Gender Dysphoria." *Journal of Sex Education and Therapy* 24, no. 3: 128–36.

Chaing, Howard. 2012. *Transgender China*. New York: Palgrave Macmillan.

Cohen-Kettenis, Peggy T., and Friedemann Pfäfflin. 2010. "The DSM Diagnostic Criteria for Gender Identity Disorder in Adolescents and Adults." *Archives of Sexual Behavior* 39, no. 2: 499–513.

Colebunders, Britt, Griet De Cuypere, and Stan Monstrey. 2015. "New Criteria for Sex Reassignment Surgery: WPATH Standards of Care, Version 7, Revisited." *International Journal of Transgenderism* 16, no. 4: 222–33. doi.org/10.1080/15532739.2015.1081086.

Coleman, Eli, et al. 2012. "Standards of Care for the Health of Transsexual, Transgender, and Gender-Nonconforming People, Version 7." *International Journal of Transgenderism* 13, no. 4: 165–232.

De Cuypere, Griet, Gail Knudson, and Walter O. Bockting. 2010. "Response of the World Professional Association for Transgender Health to the Proposed *DSM 5* Criteria for Gender Incongruence." *International Journal of Transgenderism* 12, no. 2: 119–23.

Ehrbar, Randall D. 2011. *Case Study of a Transition from "Male to Not-Male" or "Male to Eunuch" (MtE)*. Paper presented at the Twenty-Second WPATH Biennial Symposium, Atlanta, September 24–28.

Ehrbar, Randall D., and R. Nicholas Gorton. 2011. "Exploring Provider Treatment Models in Interpreting the Standards of Care." *International Journal of Transgenderism* 12, no. 4: 198–210.

Ehrensaft, Diane. 2016. *The Gender Creative Child: Pathways for Nurturing and Supporting Children Who Live Outside Gender Boxes*. New York: Experiment Publishing.

Empire Blue Cross Blue Shield. 2017. "Clinical UM Guidelines: Sex Reassignment Surgery." Guideline #CG-SURG-27, effective August 17. www.empireblue.com/medicalpolicies /guidelines/gl_pw_a051166.htm.

Ettner, Randi, Stan Monstrey, and Eli Coleman, eds. 2016. *Principles of Transgender Medicine and Surgery*. New York: Haworth.

Gijs, Luk, and Anne Brewaeys. 2007. "Surgical Treatment of Gender Dysphoria in Adults and Adolescents: Recent Developments, Effectiveness, and Challenges." *Annual Review of Sex Research* 18, no. 1: 178–224.

Hage, J. J., and R. B. Karim. 2000. "Ought GIDNOS Get Nought? Treatment Options for Nontranssexual Gender Dysphoria." *Plastic Reconstructive Surgery* 105, no. 3: 1222–27.

Hembree, Wylie C., et al. 2017. "Endocrine Treatment of Gender-Dysphoric/Gender-Incongruent Persons: An Endocrine Society Clinical Practice Guideline." *Journal of Clinical Endocrinology and Metabolism* 102, no. 11: 3869–3903. doi.org/10.1210/jc.2017-01658.

Iowa Civil Rights Commission. 2016. "Sexual Orientation and Gender Identity: An Employers' Guide to Iowa Law Compliance." icrc.iowa.gov/sites/default/files/publications/2016 /SOGIEmpl.pdf (accessed January 11, 2018).

Johnson T. W., and M. J. Irwig. 2014. "What's Missing? The Hidden World of Castration and Testicular Self-Injury among Eunuchs." *Nature Reviews/Urology* 11, no. 5: 297–300.

Johnson, T. W., and R. J. Wassersug. 2010. "Gender Identity Disorder outside the Binary: When Gender Identity Disorder-Not Otherwise Specified Is Not Good Enough." *Archives of Sexual Behavior* 39, 597–98.

Knudson, Gail, Griet De Cuypere, and Walter Bockting. 2010. "Recommendations for Revision of the DSM Diagnoses of Gender Identity Disorders: Consensus Statement of the World Professional Association for Transgender Health." *International Journal of Transgenderism* 12, no. 2: 115–18.

Krieger, Irwin. 2017. *Counseling Transgender and Non-binary Youth*. London: Jessica Kingsley.

Lev, Arlene I. 2004. *Transgender Emergence: Therapeutic Guidelines for Working with Gender Variant People and Their Families*. New York: Haworth Clinical Practice.

Levin, Stephen, et al. 1998. *The Standards of Care for Gender Identity Disorders*. 5th version. Harry Benjamin International Gender Dysphoria Association.

Meyer, Walter, et al. 2001. "The Harry Benjamin Gender Dysphoria Association's Standards of Care for Gender Identity Disorders, Sixth Version." *Journal of Psychology and Human Sexuality* 13, no. 1: 1–30.

Meyerowitz, Joanne. 2004. *How Sex Changed: A History of Transsexuality in the United States.* Cambridge, MA: Harvard University Press.

Murad, Mohammad Hassan, et al. 2010. "Hormonal Therapy and Sex Reassignment: A Systematic Review and Meta-analysis of Quality of Life and Psychosocial Outcomes." *Clinical Endocrinology* 72, no. 2: 214–31.

National Center for Transgender Equality. 2018. *Know Your Rights.* transequality.org/know-your -rights (accessed January 11).

Pfäfflin, Friedemann, and Astrid Junge. 1998. "Sex Reassignment: Thirty Years of International Follow-up Studies after Sex Reassignment Surgery: A Comprehensive Review, 1961–1991." *International Journal of Transgenderism.* web.archive.org/web/20070503090247/http://www .symposion.com/ijt/pfaefflin/1000.htm.

Rachlin, Katherine. 1999. "Factors Which Influence Individual's Decisions When Considering FTM Genital Surgery." *International Journal of Transgenderism* 3, no. 3. web.archive.org /web/20070218152435/http://www.symposion.com:80/ijt/ijt990302.htm.

Rachlin, Katherine, Cecilia Dhejne, and George R. Brown. 2010. "The Future of GID NOS in the DSM-V: Report of the GID NOS Working Group of the WPATH GID Consensus Process." *International Journal of Transgenderism* 12, no. 2: 86–93.

Segal, Corrine. 2016. "Oregon Court Rules That 'Nonbinary' Is a Legal Gender." *PBS Newshour Online,* June 11. www.pbs.org/newshour/rundown/oregon-court-rules-that-nonbinary -is-a-legal-gender/.

Singh, Anneliese, and lore m. dickey, eds. 2017. *Affirmative Counseling and Psychological Practice with Transgender and Gender Nonconforming Clients.* Washington, DC: American Psychological Association.

Spade, Dean. 2003. "Resisting Medicine, Re/modeling Gender." *Berkeley Women's Law Journal* 18, no. 1: 15–37.

Transgender Legal Defense and Education Fund. 2018. "Press Releases." www.transgenderlegal.org /press_index.php (accessed January 11, 2018).

Vale, Kayla, et al. 2010. "The Development of Standards of Care for Individuals with a Male-to-Eunuch Gender Identity Disorder." *International Journal of Transgenderism* 12, no. 1: 40–51.

van Anders, Sari M., Nicholas L. Caverly, and Michelle Marie Johns. 2014. "Newborn Bio/logics and US Legal Requirements for Changing Gender/Sex Designations on State Identity Documents." *Feminism and Psychology* 24, no. 2: 172–92.

Wheeler, Connie Christine, and Leah Cahan Schaefer. 1984. "The Nonsurgery True Transsexual (Benjamin's Category IV): A Theoretical Rationale." In *International Research in Sexology,* vol. 1 of *Sexual Medicine,* edited by Harold I. Lief and Zwi Hoch, 167–74. New York: Praeger.

When Building a Better Vulva, Timing Is Everything

A Personal Experience with the Evolution of MTF Genital Surgery

SANDRA MESICS

Abstract Gender confirmation surgery for the MTF individual has evolved and improved over time, particularly in terms of form and function. While initially surgeons concentrated on creating a vulva that functioned for receptive penetrative intercourse, in time consumer demand and improved surgical techniques have resulted in a vulva that is esthetically pleasing, functional, and sensate. This first-person account shows how techniques evolved in a critical two-year period between 1974 and 1976.

Keywords transgender, MTF surgery, transgender surgery history

I n high school, I wanted an electric guitar. I didn't have much of a budget, so the vaunted Fender Stratocaster was not even on my radar. Even a Sears Silvertone solid body was a stretch. Fortunately, in the late 1960s, the market was flooded with Japanese imports. I ended up with a Telestar hollow body, with a single pickup. I think I paid $25 for it, and I put together my own amplifier. The Telestar's action was about as hard as an acoustic guitar's, so my fingertip calluses were maintained. It was hard to keep in tune, though the tone wasn't too bad.

It had the form of an electric guitar and some of the function as well, not unlike the state of surgically created female genitalia surgeons could offer in the late 1960s and early 1970s. The form was pretty much there, but the function? That remained to be seen.

In 1974, I was looking for a surgeon to do my sex reassignment surgery (SRS). By then, I had been on hormones for two years, was well into electrolysis, and was beginning my one-year "real life test" of living full-time in my chosen female gender. Since I was living in Philadelphia, the logical choice was the gender

TSQ: Transgender Studies Quarterly ∗ Volume 5, Number 2 ∗ May 2018
DOI 10.1215/23289252-4348672 © 2018 Duke University Press

identity clinic at Pennsylvania Hospital. They functioned much like the legendary Johns Hopkins program: candidates for SRS entered into their gatekeeping system, were seen by psychiatrists, and, if given approval, moved on to have surgery at Pennsylvania Hospital—the oldest hospital in the United States.

Dr. A. James Morgan was the psychiatrist who functioned as gatekeeper. His job was to screen out individuals who were schizophrenic or had other underlying conditions that were manifesting as a desire to change sex. He was also collecting data. I remember being given a battery of tests: the Rorschach, Minnesota Multiphasic Personality Inventory, the Bem Sex-Role Inventory, IQ, to name a few. Morgan subsequently revealed that "most of the time, psychological testing shows role diffusion, sexual identity problems, and the idealization of femininity as an abstract concept" (1978: 279). Over time, we developed a rapport during our sessions: I began to feel comfortable with him and came to believe that he really was there to assure I wasn't making a mistake.

Now, in those pre-Internet, pre–social media days, we had a thriving underground network of transsexual people. We shared our stories and found out who the willing hormone providers were, which electrologists to avoid, which surgeons did the best work, and, most importantly, what to tell the psychiatrists if you wanted to be approved for surgery. You told them you hated your penis. You told them you liked men. You told them that you just wanted to blend in with society as a woman, get married, and settle down.

Herein lay the problem for me: I was at best ambivalent about my penis. I liked women and, in fact, was married to one when I started to transition. I had very limited sexual experience in general, and even more limited experience with men. As to blending in, and settling down in society, I really didn't have a problem with that.

So what to tell Dr. Morgan? I thought that if he were really there to help me, I had to be honest with him. So I told him that after surgery, I would likely be lesbian. So there! While I half expected to be booted out of the program, he just said, "OK, let's explore that." And so we proceeded. He encouraged me to further explore my sexuality, to experiment with men, and verify that I still wanted to proceed down the path leading to surgery. I took his advice, and of course, it didn't change anything. My feelings were validated.

As it turned out, Dr. Morgan was one of the more progressive psychiatrists in the day. He often recommended that his MTF patients attend women's consciousness-raising groups to get a more realistic view of womanhood. He felt that about 30 percent of candidates were struggling with homophobia caused by social stigma rather than gender-identity issues, thus the recommendation of experimenting with gay sex. A large proportion of his clients had "inadequate personality," which needed further psychotherapy. He was interested in the holistic care of the trans person: "Before we embark on the mission of helping the male-to-female transsexual to be a woman or the female-to-male transsexual to be a man, we must begin to explore the necessity of the candidate to develop as a person—no small task for anyone" (Morgan 1978: 283).

At the Pennsylvania Hospital program, candidates for surgery had to be "more than 21 years old, a transsexual for at least 3 years, cross dressing for more than 1 year and taking female hormones for at least 9 months. In addition, the patient cannot be married" (Malloy, Noone, and Morgan 1976: 335). So my spouse and I proceeded with a divorce, and I was good to go. Dr. Morgan signed me off for surgery, and so I went off to meet the surgical team: urologist Dr. Terrence Malloy and plastic surgeon Dr. R. Barrett Noone.

Now, to digress a moment, discovering which surgeons did good work was a large part of the underground transsexual social network. We listened intently to the experiences of our "sisters" who had undergone surgical procedures. If we were lucky, the information was firsthand. If not, it was garnered second- or thirdhand. We exchanged information at regional meetings of organizations such as the United Transvestite Transsexual Society (UTTS) or one of the Transvestite Independence Clubs. The Transsexual Action Organization (TAO) disseminated some information through personal correspondence or their publications *Mirage* and *Moonshadow*. Because I was a regional director of TAO and an editor of various transvestite/transsexual publications (*Image, Female Impersonator News*, and others), I was able to gather and disseminate some of this information myself. Those of us on the East Coast were able to get more information on East Coast surgeons, but some of our contacts had surgery on the West Coast or in such exotic places as Casablanca with the pioneer surgeon Dr. Georges Burou.

For instance, the consensus was to stay away from Dr. John Ronald Brown in California because, while his fee was low, his outcomes were not always good. Dr. Roberto Granato in New York had pretty good results in creating a deep vagina, but the trade-off was often a large skin graft from the thigh. It was commonly held that the genital surgery performed at Johns Hopkins was esthetically pleasing and functional, but they were doing fewer and fewer. Dr. Benito Rish in New York was reported to do some pretty good genital surgery, but he far excelled at facial surgery. But what was the feedback about the Pennsylvania Hospital team? A good friend of mine had surgery there, and esthetically the work was pretty good, and there was some depth to the vagina, but sensation? Not so much.

For MTF trans patients in the late 1960s and early 1970s, the focus for the surgeons was on creating a functioning vagina and an esthetically pleasing vulva. "The ideal surgical procedure to construct female genitalia . . . should . . . produce an adequate vagina for intercourse and have a cosmetic result that is virtually indistinguishable from a normal female subject" (Malloy, Noone, and Morgan

1976: 337). The focus was on the constructed vagina's ability to accommodate a penis for intercourse. In fact, it was not until 1976 that surgeons made "a more formal attempt" to create an innervated neoclitoris as opposed to a cosmetic swelling that was meant to resemble a clitoris (Goddard, Vickery, and Terry 2007: 986). My dilemma was threefold: I probably wouldn't be using my new vagina for a lot of receptive intercourse, I really would have liked to have an orgasm now and then, and having a clitoris was not a common option in 1976. I was starting to get cold feet.

Things didn't get any better when I met the surgical team. They were at best cold and dismissive, and when I asked about sensation, they were very noncommittal and almost insulted that I dared ask about that. They threw a sheet at me so that I could cover my bottom while they did a cursory exam, and said that they could get me in for surgery in three weeks. I was simultaneously excited that my goal was in sight but still nagged about what the outcome might be.

For whatever reason, fate intervened.

About ten days prior to surgery, I unexpectedly broke out in hives. They covered my body, and my eyes swelled shut. I was taken to the emergency department at Pennsylvania Hospital where I was stabilized, and some labs were drawn. A few days later, the lab results revealed that I had hepatitis. The ensuing jaundice left no doubt about the diagnosis. Surgery and even estrogen was off the table for a year. I was devastated, both physically and emotionally. As the acute phase of the illness set in, I tried to get admitted to hospitals in Philadelphia, but they wouldn't accept my health insurance. I returned to my childhood home, to be cared for by my mother and aunt.

For a couple of weeks, the only time I was able to get out of bed was to use the bathroom and wash up. Just doing that exhausted me for the rest of the day. I was far too ill to think about anything clearly. Constant headaches, nausea, and fatigue kept me from contemplating life without hormones or sex reassignment surgery. Gradually and steadily, I improved, and after three months I was back at work. As my health returned, so did unwanted erections at odd times, a constant reminder of life without estrogen. Needless to say, breast development and sensitivity also stopped as well.

These unwanted changes reinforced my conviction that I needed to undergo SRS. In fact, they seemed to strengthen my resolve that life as a man was not workable for me. Was I depressed? You bet. Did I feel cheated? Again, yes. But when self-medicating with alcohol or drugs was off the table for the year, the only alternative was to get healthy and cross days off the calendar until my time in exile was up.

I had heard of Dr. David Wesser, a New York plastic surgeon, who had been a military surgeon in Vietnam. His reputation was that sometimes his vaginas were not the deepest, but he created a clitoris. When I had recovered and been back on estrogen for a few months, in mid-1976, I had a consult with him. He confirmed that he did create a clitoris, and while he couldn't guarantee the results, in most of his over three hundred cases, his patients were orgasmic following surgery. This was welcome news, but more than that, I had a good feeling that I had found another compassionate provider.

In describing his surgical technique, Wesser stated, "The small V-shaped skin flap is sutured in hood-fashion at the apex of the meatus to simulate a clitoris. A small triangle of intact spongiosum is deliberately left beneath this to afford some erotic sensation" (1978: 310–11). In a discussion of Wesser's outcomes, the pioneering SRS surgeon Dr. Milton Edgerton commented, "The main variation that we have made in our procedure in the last year [1977] has been introduction of techniques to construct a clitoris . . . because the patients are beginning to ask that we do so" (Wesser 1978: 318). As time went by, techniques improved, according to Plemons (2013) partly because of advances in microsurgical techniques, and partly because of how the female body should experience pleasure. In Malloy's technique, sensitive tissue from the penile glans was inverted to become the "cervix" at the end of the vaginal canal. Stimulation of this neocervix could lead to orgasm, but only through some form of penetration. By this time, the concept of a vaginal orgasm for cisgender females was being challenged, and the clitoris was recognized as the center of sexual pleasure in women. Pioneering surgeons such as Edgerton and Wesser recognized that the glans penis was homologous to the clitoris and so pioneered the creation of a sensate clitoris to provide the patient with as "real" a female orgasm as possible. I would add that other drivers of improved surgical techniques were patient expectations like mine driving demand and, eventually, another generation of surgeons who are themselves transgender individuals.

In August 1976, I had surgery with Dr. Wesser in Yonkers, New York. It entailed a hospital stay of five days and a couple of follow-up office visits. Postoperative care in those days was minimal. I had my urinary catheter removed a week after surgery in Dr. Wesser's Manhattan office, and I immediately went back to Philadelphia with instructions to go to an emergency room if I was unable to void by the next day. Pain was controlled with oral Percodan (oxycodone and aspirin). I initially recovered at my ex-spouse's apartment, where she gave me watchful but emotionally disconnected care. After two weeks, I was off medication and moved into a tiny efficiency apartment in Center City, Philadelphia. With my new anatomy and new domicile, I started a new phase of life. While I was looking forward to this new independence, I was also sadly aware that I was living alone for the first time in my life.

In those days, Dr. Wesser had his postoperative patients wear their vaginal stents pretty much continuously for the first couple of months. This was such a nuisance, as it had to be held in place by a panty girdle and a thick sanitary pad. Despite this confinement, on one occasion it did manage to slip out of its confines and make its way down my pant leg, while I was walking down a street in Philadelphia. I decorously slipped into a storefront doorway, retrieved it from my ankle, and put it in my handbag. Otherwise it resided inside my neovagina more or less all the time.

A couple of months later, while becoming acquainted with my new anatomy, I discovered that Dr. Wesser's technique of creating a clitoris worked very well. The orgasm was not unlike what I was used to. As it turned out, my two-year enforced hiatus resulted in a more pleasurable outcome.

It would seem that timing was everything, especially in the historical context of having a better vulva. And for all trans women, the world has become a little better as surgeons continue to develop improved techniques—creating Fender Stratocasters where once were only Telestar hollow bodies.

Sandra Mesics is director of St. Luke's School of Nursing in Bethlehem, Pennsylvania. She has taught maternal-newborn nursing and practiced as a registered nurse in labor and delivery and as a certified nurse-midwife, including providing transgender care. An early transgender activist, she was Philadelphia director of the Transsexual Action Organization (TAO) and an early organizer for the United Transvestite Transsexual Society (UTTS). She edited and published *Image Magazine*, an early transgender quarterly, and was author and editor of many transgender publications for Neptune Productions. She earned a BS degree in psychology from Pennsylvania State University, a BSN from Barry University, and an MSN from the University of Miami.

References

Goddard, Jonathan C., Richard M. Vickery, and Tim R. Terry. 2007. "Development of Feminizing Genitoplasty for Gender Dysphoria." *Journal of Sexual Medicine*, no. 4: 981–89.

Malloy, Terrence R., R. Barrett Noone, and A. James Morgan. 1976. "Experience with the One-Stage Surgical Approach for Constructing Female Genitalia in Male Transsexuals." *Journal of Urology* 116, no. 3: 335–37.

Morgan, A. James. 1978. "Psychotherapy for Transsexual Candidates Screened Out of Surgery." *Archives of Sexual Behavior* 7, no. 4: 273–83.

Plemons, Eric D. 2013. "It Is as It Does: Genital Form and Function in Sex Reassignment Surgery." *Journal of Medical Humanities* 35, no. 1: 37–55. doi.org/10.1007/s10912-013-9267-z.

Wesser, David R. 1978. "A Single Stage Operative Technique for Castration, Vaginal Construction, and Perineoplasty in Transsexuals." *Archives of Sexual Behavior* 7, no. 4: 309–23.

Busting Out

Happenstance Surgery, Clinic Effects, and the Poetics of Genderqueer Subjectivity

J. HORNCASTLE

Abstract This article approaches transgender surgery from the "side door" and explores the consequences of happenstance surgery for the gender-nonnormative subject. In this happenstance context, the trans chest as a concept is problematic on two counts — being popularly understood only in the cis-surgical context of cancer treatment (mastectomy) or the FTM transitional context (of top surgery). Neither of these contexts readily allows for a nonnormative trans chest. The author utilizes their own experiences of chest surgery to critique delegitimizing, prohibitive clinic practices that efface or misrecognize gender-diverse subjectivity. While this critique is straightforward in that it highlights the need for ongoing change in medical care practices, the author advances a philosophical analysis of genderqueer subjectivity that turns toward a poetics of selfhood. They suggest that understanding the poetics of genderqueerness displaces the "big P" politics of alterity that commonly marks queer activism. They argue that this displacement has epistemological value for what they call trans-peripheral surgical subjects. Building on notions of burdensome self-advocacy and the possibility of being, the article posits that the poetics of nonnormativity acts as a stabilizing or restorative feature of genderqueer and trans-peripheral life. This is especially linked to experiences of surgical transformation in hospitals and surgical clinics that contribute to and shape existential stress. Beginning with a contextualization of genderqueerness and an explanation of the terms *trans-peripheral* and *queer*, the article moves from a narrative account of surgical experience to a theory that grounds poetics as a complement to the politics of selfhood.
Keywords breast clinic, genderqueer, poetics, trans chest, trans-peripheral

> Art lasts because it gives us a language for our inner reality, and that is not a private hieroglyph; it is a connection across time to all those others who have suffered and failed, found happiness, lost it, faced death, ruin, struggled, survived, known the night-hours of inconsolable pain.
> —Jeanette Winterson, *Shafts of Sunlight*

TSQ: Transgender Studies Quarterly ★ Volume 5, Number 2 ★ May 2018   **251**
DOI 10.1215/23289252-4348684   © 2018 Duke University Press

First. Person.

Speaking to my own experience with breast cancer[1] and ensuing double mastectomy serves the purpose of illuminating an epistemology of genderqueer selfhood and animating a theoretical engagement with questions of alterity and subjectivity. The first-person expression of trans-peripheral subjectivity is viewed for what it specifically reveals about institutional contexts of surgical experiences *and* the subjectivity of selfhood; these are two directions I follow in this article. My account of "self" is intersectional and ultimately self-centered as all accounts of self must be, but it is not truly solipsistic.[2] My aim is to look outward from the self and sharpen the analytical lens through which the subjectivity of genderqueer trans-peripherality can be explored.

For people who identify as genderqueer or butch, or who identify on a masculine spectrum, or who trouble neat gender identifications by situating the gendered self along an "incoherent" collocation of masculine and feminine scales (see Noble 2006; Macdonald 2013), the mastectomy opportunity—as a masculine chest opportunity—can present itself as a kind of top surgery, through the side door. In this sense, which I call "trans-peripheral," the surgery is procured as a by-product of disease.

The surgical outcome of a masculine trans chest can be achieved through different paths, and in this article I raise the profile of one such path. I ruefully note that a cancer treatment route may also displace the hyper-regulated psycho-surgical interventionist route that approves transition in normative FTM transition contexts. While acknowledging the struggles many trans people have in public health and gender pathologizing contexts, it is important to note that all public health-care forms of surgery are gatekept by medical professionals.

Without identifying within a female-to-male (FTM) transition space, and seeking what is colloquially referred to as "top surgery" (mastectomy and chest reshaping/sculpting in line with a masculine aesthetic), I had not, as a person with breasts identifying as a female-born genderqueer person, sought to surgically procure such a chest.[3] However, the opportunity for chest shaping to my own gender ideals (although contingent as described below) occurred when treatment for breast cancer eventually led to a double mastectomy. Before moving on to an account of my route to a trans chest, I will briefly explain how genderqueerness and trans-peripherality meet in the context of my story.

I have always been more comfortable with female masculinity than female femininity. As a child and as a younger woman, if I ever did femininity it was excruciatingly uncomfortable and often traumatic. Later, when discovering the concept of queer femme, especially through reading and admiring the seminal work of femmes like Joan Nestle (1987, 1998) and Amber Hollibaugh (2000), I could apply those new ways of thinking to a freer lived experience. Other femme texts (see for example, Duggan and McHugh 1996; Brushwood Rose and

Camilleri 2002; Volcano and Dahl 2008) further increased my understanding of gender flexibility. But queer femme was still discomforting as a subjective experience unless my femmeness was adopted part-time. Doing femme, albeit as a powerful plaything, felt safe and fun within queer and trans subcultural contexts; this allowed me to draw upon and explore the ludic qualities of hyperfemininity. However, within these exhilarating discoveries, I was yet to find a comfortable, less whimsical gender feeling. Now if I do femme, I do it as selfconscious drag. Likewise, transgender butch and identification on the transmasculine spectrum (see Halberstam 1998) have also encouraged me to keep seeking a comfortable, mundane gender feeling. By this I mean a satisfying synchronicity of emotional, self-conscious, psychological, embodied, and performed aspects of self that are sensed. Sonny Nordmarken also refers to this as feeling gender: "We, as shape-shifters, resist abjection by making our own selves. In so doing, we question and deconstruct dominant epistemologies, which assume the existence of an essential 'self.' We acknowledge that ideas of what constitutes the human and how we know this are just ideas. We create trans epistemologies, which locate authority to know in the *feeling* about our gendered selves" (2014: 42). Although I do not wholeheartedly agree that the making of a self necessarily engages with a resistance to *abjection* (I argue this point below), I do suggest that the emphasis on feeling can lead away from an explicit politics of being, toward a poetics of being. This ties in with my understanding that genderqueerness does not have to mean baldly wearing the "big P" politics or megaphone politics of identity activism, or the "big S" sexuality of sex radicalism. This is not to say I do not treasure those activisms; my point is that that there are ways to sit by or move alongside them. The importance of feeling is especially sharp in genderqueer and trans-peripheral surgical contexts in which the becoming of self is at stake, and with Nordmarken I prioritize feeling and reject an emphasis on an essential self.

A feeling I focus attention on shortly is that of being "at home." I do not associate this feeling with a place of stasis or monolithic fixity; instead I prioritize a condition of home—comfort—enabled through the poetics of one's gendered self, wherever that may be, and as Nordmarken says, with authority in feeling (42). I have been (for decades of my life) enacting a search for a comfortably gendered self, and it has been through a conceptualization of queerness, of adopting a queer sensibility, that my selfhood has felt real, and close to home.

My life has been hampered and overshadowed by surviving gender violence, and, for me, the necessity of becoming possible is inflected by my understanding of queerness as a sensibility. This was shaped by such theorists as Eve K. Sedgwick (1993), Judith Butler (1993, 2004), Ann Cvetkovich (1995), Michael Warner (1993, 1999), Robert McRuer (1997, 2003, 2006), and José Muñoz (2009), who all provided ways of understanding queer*ness* that can run beyond sexual politics to a sensibility of alterity that includes and shifts the parameters of ethics, politics, poetry, and the subjectivity of selfhood. More recently, I find that the intersections of queer theory and crip-culture (see Clare 1999, 2003; Sandhal 2003), the social science of medicine (see Stacey and Bryson 2012), and mad-pride (see McNamara 2013; Spandler and Barker 2016) make the best sense of queerness (theorized as a sensibility) that relates to my own lived experiences of gender-violence survival.

I am indebted to theoretical predecessors because I benefit from the queer ideas of others who have the capacity to change my life in material, positive ways. A case in point is an example in the special queer theory issue of *differences* in 1991. In that issue, Julia Creet turned the tables of a feminist debate about s/m practices. Instead of asking "whether s/m is politically feminist," she asked "how feminism may function within the economy of a lesbian s/m fantasy" (1991: 136). The effect of this reversal, although in Creet's framing it is of a sexuality issue, speaks to my point about "big P" politics. Creet says:

> This reversal also effects a displacement out of the realm of politics, that which is considered to be the most "real," and into the realm of fantasy, that which is considered to be the most "unreal." In the end I hope to have shown how the unreal and the real are implicated in each other; that is, how the imagination can have a pervasive force in politics, and how politics can influence the realm and the boundaries of fantasy. (136)

For me the boundaries of politics intersect with imagination, fantasy, myth, poetry, the unnatural (conceptual places where queer subjectivity coheres), and I have criss-crossed those boundaries in my desire for a trans chest. My queer masculinity is idiosyncratic to the point of incoherence in broader settings (institutional, social, and public realms), but incoherence in normative settings is still attached to the real (as Creet says, reversely) and is not the same as unintelligibility all round. The term *genderqueer* remains, after years of use, the one that best unfetters me from gender designations of others that I cannot comfortably utilize.

From Breast to Chest—Happenstance and Procurement

The two options (cancer mastectomy and FTM mastectomy) raise an issue of terminology. *Trans chest* may refer to the chest of someone who has transitioned or is transitioning from male to female or female to male. Using the example of FTM, this often requires the firm distinction of sex/gender referents, male and female, and speaks to the prefix *trans*, meaning transition from/to binarized gender positions, from woman to man. It is important to avoid assuming that people who transition necessarily or always seek normative gender configurations, while acknowledging that there is a depth and coherence to the term *FTM. Trans chest* may also refer to the chest of a woman who transforms her body *without* transitioning from female to male and moves within a masculine part of the gender spectrum. The term *trans chest*, as I use it in this article, is linked to this complexity of gender movement. My use of *trans chest* and *trans-peripheral* relies on this distinction between normative and nonnormative notions of transition.

When my options for cancer treatment became necessarily surgical, moving through invasive investigations, multiple excisions, and a single mastectomy, I faced unique issues that this happenstance presented. I rejected the default, gender-normative procedure of a postcancer breast reconstruction on one side of my chest. My first difficulty as a gender-diverse cancer patient was about how to negotiate the default options presented to me and challenge heteronormative binary gender assumptions that were embedded in hospital care practices.

Questions of agency impacted my ability to argue for my ideal surgical outcome, a masculine-looking chest. One recourse toward this ideal was to request a double mastectomy. This request was made strategically within the parameters of prophylaxis. It was easier for me to appeal to the legitimacy of cancer fear (not my own) that is accommodated by medical professionals who themselves are entrenched within, and constitutive of, the dominant fear and fight discourses around cancer. My double mastectomy was sanctioned (and carried out) on the grounds of fear of cancer rather than body modification in line with my genderqueer preferences.[4]

The opportunity for a bone fide trans chest came serendipitously some years later with a different breast cancer surgeon who was cognizant of, and open to using, terms such as *cis, transgender, chest-aesthetics,* and *contouring.* Notably, I was in a more self-present, hypercognitive state, which meant I was better able to articulate and express myself. However, even then, this agency was compromised by the contingencies and relations of the clinic that subordinate the patient to the gaze of the doctor. One can feel so very overexposed and diminished in medical clinic settings, and I had to be my own hero in the clinic if I wanted *my* ideal chest. In "Slow Death," when Lauren Berlant suggests "we need better ways to talk about activities oriented toward the reproduction of ordinary life: the burdens of compelled will that exhaust people" (2007: 757), she speaks directly to the problem of a capacity to act for oneself in trying circumstances (for me this relates to clinic experiences). Her point is that "a manifest lack of self-cultivating attention can easily be recast as irresponsibility, shallowness, resistance, refusal or incapacity," and, as a result, "just being different can be read as a heroic placeholder for resistance to something, affirmation of something, or a transformative desire" (757). I did feel "burdened" by a sense of required resistant heroism. Against this burden, the importance of my trans chest felt greatly displaced by the difficulties of having a clinic conversation. I borrowed the coherence of FTM top surgery so that my breast cancer surgeon could at least understand the ballpark I was in (another reason I use the term *trans-peripheral*), and this was a strategic deferral to a common language. But I also had in mind the words and imagery of Raphael Campo and Gary Fisher, who have beautifully articulated negative clinic effects in their poetry (see Campo 1997, 1999; Fisher 1996). I imagined Gary and Raphael in the clinic with me as ghosts, and we shared my moment of "slow death," to stay with Berlant's terminology for a moment. In this way I progressed through my time in the clinic, employing a form of what Berlant calls "lateral agency" (2007), in which my deteriorated sense of self could let go of heroism (adept self-advocating agency) and just "be."

My trans-chest luck was surgeon specific, too. Many breast oncology surgeons are still invested in the default option of breast reconstruction "for women" who are assumed to embrace femininity and feminine gender identity (see, for example, Ng et al. 2016; Fitzal and Schrenk 2015). The work of Jain (2007b) is significant in this regard, providing one of the very few butch-specific narratives and critiques of breast cancer care that falls outside gender norms. One of my annual breast cancer clinic reviews was serendipitous because the surgeon had some understanding of gender complexity. Articulating the notion of a trans chest that was different from, but similar to, FTM top surgery *was* legitimized, and I was referred to plastics for my trans chest.

Procurement

This shift to plastics raises an important issue about the intersections of sex-gender surgery (breast specific) and aesthetics. Within a post–breast cancer context, there is a magnanimity about surgical restoration. The construction of breasts after a mastectomy is not and has never been a treatment for cancer; it is sex/gender treatment through body modification. I have always found it odd that this should be left literally in the hands of breast oncology and plastic surgeons who are not gender-spectrum aware or critically analytical of gender in its many forms, or, more importantly, trained and educated to engage so fundamentally in the gender vulnerability of others. However, this system seems to work well for many women who are perhaps not so needful of being critical about the postcancer breast-reconstruction process. I venture to say, though, that even these women may benefit from a less routinized process, one that invests much more time in gender in all its complexity. This could be done in workshops and structured group learning environments (without pathologizing people or ushering them to psychological counseling services as the only means to talk about gender complexity).[5]

Many women feel troubled or traumatized by the removal of breasts, especially when breasts are seen as integral to femininity, sexuality, and womanliness. And, as I recognize, many women happily go through the process of surgical breast reconstruction performed by a breast oncology/plastic surgeon.

I do not argue against this being a positive thing for many gender-normative folk. My point is that the reconstructed chest in my own example, as a trans chest, does not fall into this popular paradigm, and another paradigm does not exist.[6]

Encouragingly, when my requested chest surgery (as a departure from the female femininity of postcancer breast reconstruction) did fall under the jurisdiction of general plastics, this became an opportunity to create (at least partially by voicing my gender preferences) conditions for a genderqueer paradigm where there seemed to be none. However, this opportunity was double edged and difficult to manage. Although the plastic surgeon was immersed in the language of scar revision and body shaping—the arrangement of flesh on any ("neutral") body—she articulated an explicit ignorance of nonnormative or nonbinary gender and requested that I teach her about it. Gender, in this context, was magnified through objectification, and my plastic surgeon was intensely earnest.

As with the breast oncology surgeon, I could explain what I wanted in compromised language such as "male-looking chest" or "like an FTM chest" (indeed it was this that drove the referral); but in terms of being more specific, my language was steered by an expectation of heuristic benevolence. In this new (plastics) environment, and typical of other breast clinic experiences, I stuttered and fumbled, felt hypersensitive to exposure, and squirmed uncomfortably at the clinic effects. I said, "Well it is a little complex," and before I could utter another word, the surgeon spun around in her swivel chair, skated it over to sit directly in front of me, and said, "Give me the potted version—teach me." She opened her legs very wide, taking both mine between hers, and leaned in toward me. With a smile and an expression that mixed concern and expectance, she forthrightly set the scene for me to provide gender enlightenment. I felt overwhelmingly confined and infantilized. My narrative is not unique or new. For example, in her *Cancer Journals*, Audre Lorde spoke of losing her "moxie" (1980: 62), and in *Resisterectomy*, Chase Joynt and Mary Bryson both speak of being "boxed in," "crushed," and "invaded" by medical clinic dialogues (Joynt 2012a).

While my surgeon may have felt magnanimous about her willingness to learn from a patient (she was explicit in her request to be educated), she seemed paradoxically unconscious of the equally explicit terms of reduction that she orchestrated (for me to be potted). I was asked to define the term *queer*, and then *genderqueer*, then *trans-peripheral*. I thought that for the surgeon to understand genderqueer*ness* (as an experience of selfhood that embraces margins and oddities, and rejects norms), she would need more teaching than our quick exchange could provide. Definitions of words like *gender binary* and *spectrum* seemed inadequate, so I began to speak of people and lived experiences, explaining that there are different and personal ways that people experience their gender and that although multiple genders are becoming more widely understood, these are sometimes oversimplified as identification labels, and people's lives are still very much constrained by social mores and gender norms. I said, "If you take the example of me not wanting to have nipples made; this is part of my gender-queerness. Because I am comfortable with the rejection of a normative chest, I really don't want them." The surgeon could not make sense of this. Her reply was immediate: she detailed the two methods nipples can be made. As if she had not heard me, she said this would be like the "cherry on the cake" and in her view an ideal outcome of chest surgery. I reiterated (although my words fizzled out as I looked past my surgeon to focus on the white ceiling and the neon strip light) that my lack of nipples was something that I did not want to change.

Explaining my genderqueerness remained a conversational ideal that I failed to capitalize on. I stumbled through the fraught terrain of this conversation, and as with many clinic appointments, the exchange was funneled into the surgeon's normative framework, and I forgot to pursue my queer agenda. I did not ask about the range of scar shapes that I had thought about beforehand (embracing oddity or uniqueness, accentuating scar lines, perhaps an anchor shape, or scars that intentionally avoided the curvilinear form in favor of sharp angles and geometric lines). I felt trapped and pinned to the spot. The physical envelopment of my legs between the surgeon's acted as a metaphor for our broader knowledge exchange. She absorbed my words but avoided deep listening, and this manifest ingestion led to my effacement. Although the surgeon was open to the idea of learning (she was keen, good humored, and speaking in good faith), my capacity to teach and her capacity to learn were compromised by the constraints of the clinic.

Perhaps my example can further encourage gender-nonconforming people and their caregivers (in clinical breast cancer mastectomy contexts) to address more explicitly, positively, supportively, and bravely than I the options for chest surgery that fall outside, or exist peripherally to, standard surgical practices. Practical solutions to resolve unpleasant or harmful medical and clinical practices are important to develop (for example, using qualitative data and analysis of diversity of experience, disseminating narrated accounts, fostering support networks, and broadening the scope of education and training). Taking an oblique approach, I now turn to a philosophical consideration of the subjectivity of trans-peripheral genderqueerness that is compromised in clinic settings.

Subjectivity and Succor

My opportunity to voice queerness was a moment when queer politics could explicitly take shape, but in contexts in which the knower feels devoured rather than understood, and strong self-advocacy dissipates, where else can the non-normative subject turn for succor? By questioning how one continues to positively "be" in such contexts, I argue that although a failure to self-advocate must *not* correspond to an actual failure of selfhood (or a sense of confinement in an unreal, unknowable self), an additional thinking point extends from philosophizing gender violence to a poetics of being. To set this point out: a weakened ability to be a high-functioning political agent in surgical (formal medical) contexts should not be viewed only in terms of explicit political resistance in which one fails (flees from or loses sight of one's own agenda) or fights (experiences degrees of trauma and violence while trying to teach or explain). The capacity to continue becoming a person is always extant, and in addition to existing theories of agency (for example, Berlant's [2007] notion of "lateral" agency, or Bryson and Stacey's [2013: 197] acknowledgment of queer "artful failure"), I draw from Judith Butler here.[7] Butler speaks of nonnormative genders that are not protected from violence and are not cared for within the institutional contexts of available gender norms: "The derealization of gendered violence has implications for understanding how and why certain gender presentations are criminalized and pathologized, how subjects who cross gender risk internment and imprisonment, why violence against transgendered subjects is not recognized as violence, and why it is sometimes inflicted by the very states who should be offering such subjects protection from violence" (2004: 218). Such unrecognized violence happens in the clinic as I have described; the clinic effects are felt keenly even though gender violence is familiar to nonnormative subjects. I felt cornered. Bryson said that she felt her "body crushing" (in Joynt 2012a). Joynt relates how he was asked, "What are you? Are you a transgender?," and he sighs deeply with what appears in his video to be familiarity with a great weight of violence. This is borne literally in his body, audible as a chest-slumping exhalation (2012a).

These effects occur in a place where clinicians are designated explicitly as caregivers and are testimony to Butler's warning about laxity of protection. However, Butler continues with a comment about politics and philosophy, a bifurcation that I use to explain my turn to poetics:

> It is not a question merely of producing a new future for genders that do not yet exist. The genders I have in mind have been existing for a long time, but they have not been admitted into the terms that govern reality. It is a question of developing, within law, within psychiatry, within social and literary theory, a new legitimating lexicon for the gender complexity that we have always been living. . . . The conception of politics at work here is centrally concerned with the question of survival, of how to create a world in which those who understand their gender and their desire to be nonnormative can live and thrive not only without the threat of violence from the outside but without the pervasive sense of their own unreality, which can lead to suicide or a suicidal life. Lastly, I would ask what place the thinking of the possible has within political theorising. One can object and say, ah, but you are trying only to make gender complexity possible. (2004: 219)

To paraphrase Butler's rejoinder to the hypothetical counterargument, she stresses how such a response (a negative reaction to gender complexity) fails to consider norms and values that are measured in ways that create "good" and "bad" genders (219). Obviously, this contributes to violence, pain, discomfort, and derealization for people. The important notion of succor that I extract from Butler's response comes when she adds, "But there is a normative aspiration here, and it has to do with the ability to live and breathe and move and would no doubt belong somewhere in what is called a philosophy of freedom" (219). Such movement might be as I described at the beginning of this article; along and within a part of the gender spectrum, it might mean walking down the high street of a country town, or it might mean breathing easily in a hospital clinic. Beyond the obvious comparisons between Butler's broadly applicable comments and how they might apply in specific instances of, say, trans-peripheral genderqueer life, I suggest that what Butler gestures to as philosophy of freedom has an affiliate in poetics.

Affect (caused through effacement or reduction in the clinic, for example) can offset political tribulations because describing and being in affective states of crisis is, as I demonstrate below, suited to a poetic landscape that in turn provides succor. T. S. Eliot is apposite here. Eliot wrote in "Burnt Norton" that "human kind cannot bear very much reality" ([1943] 1971: 2), and this small line of a poem has become a lasting popular aphorism because it is so relatable. Beyond this, Eliot poeticized the crux of unbearability in other work; this can be read inspirationally (as succor) by others. Jeanette Winterson, for example, makes this explicit when she says, "Language stops the heart exploding. Or as T. S. Eliot puts it in *Murder in the Cathedral*, 'This is one moment / But know that another / shall pierce you with a sudden painful joy'" (2008). My choice of epigraph centralizes poetry as the art of the self, and as connection between troubled selves, across time and place. This links directly to how Winterson, herself inspired by Eliot, inspires others who have found succor in Winterson's poeticizing of crisis. See, for example, Amber Dawn's book, *How Poetry Saved My Life* (2013) and Audre Lorde's chapter "Poetry Is Not a Luxury," which expresses the same gratitude for poetry's function (Lorde 1984: 36–39). Lorde also remembers how a Walter de la Mare poem, which she read in her childhood, exemplified the only language she understood for *feeling* one's subjectivity of difference (1981: 714).

The poetic landscape is the antithesis of speechlessness; it provides access to further conceptualization of a rich language of becoming, out of, for example, a language of erasure or formlessness in medical clinics. In line with a "legitimating lexicon," and adding to what Butler calls "derealization" (2004: 218), are terms used by poets such as *disassembled* (edwards 2013: 321), *unbordering* (Beyer 2012), *decreation* (Carson 2005: 179), and *bodymap* (Piepzna-Samarasinha 2015: 4), among countless others. In addition to the value of a poetic language of self-creation,

I highlight below poet Mark Doty's turn to "description" (2010) as a form of becoming. I cast this as succor for those nonnormative-gender subjects who must survive gender violence by understanding themselves, through description, to be undeniably real and possible. Thus centralizing succor branches away from "big P" politics. I underpin this with a claim from Butler that "the thought of a possible life is only an indulgence for those who already know themselves to be possible. For those who are still looking to become possible, possibility is a necessity" (2004: 219).

Poetics as Homing

There are two forms of poetics that I highlight. One is about utility, and the other is about sensibility. I draw on poetry itself (the written or spoken artifacts, the poems) *and* lived contexts that lend themselves to poetic conceptualization of genderqueer subjectivity. Articulations of becoming have all been used by poets and theorists interested in existence at the margins of human being. "Becoming" is resonant in transition contexts (particularly surgical) in which nonnormativity is queer or peripheral to norms.

In 1993 Susan Stryker presented a performance of queer trans gender for a conference on rage at California State University, San Marcos. In the published text, "My Words to Victor Frankenstein above the Village of Chamounix—Performing Transgender Rage" (Stryker 1994), which adapted this performance, Stryker included a segment from a journal entry that spoke of pain, frustration, anger, and the prices paid for achieving gender visibility and intelligibility. She cast these prices as collateral to ongoing invisibility, which is "maddeningly difficult to bear" (243). At this point in the text, Stryker lays out, in raw, vivid description, the foundations for rage that culminate in her own rebirth. Significantly, this takes on poetic form, and it is in a poem on rage that the excruciation of being gender nonconforming becomes transformed. The following excerpt flows directly out of the prose:

> I cannot be, and yet—an excruciating impossibility—I am. I will do anything not to be here.

> *I will swim forever.*
> *I will die for eternity.*
> *I will learn to breathe water.*
> *I will become the water.*
> *If I cannot change my situation I will change myself.*

> In this act of magical transformation
> I recognize myself again. (247)

It is not for nothing that Stryker's now famous words to Victor Frankenstein are so enduring. Twenty-three years after it was written, her text ranked as one of the top fifteen "most-read articles of 2017" in the Duke University Press journals archive (Duke University Press 2017). Stryker's words apply across theory and prose, analysis and description, trans and queer and enraged subjectivities,[8] the political and the poetic, the desperate and the joyful, the established and the new. Here then, we see another use of the poetic. The allure of Stryker's text is due to, at least in part, this usefulness to others. Also, it is in poetry that the most sensitive distillations of human being are articulated, and when Stryker says, "I recognize myself again" (247), we know that an interrupted self has been homed and celebrated. This signals a thriving of being. For nonnormative people, poetic articulations give voice to a sense of being home, of celebrating one's realness, of recognizing a possibility to "be."

Doty speaks of recognition as a poetic art, and as freedom from speechlessness. In his book *The Art of Description*, Doty explains the connection between poetry, self, and world experience:

> At that instant when language seems to match experience, some rift is healed, some rupture momentarily salved in what Hart Crane called "the silken skilled transmemberment of song." What a word, *transmemberment*. . . . I think of it as a kind of fusion between the word and the world, one becoming—at least in "one floating instant," to paraphrase Crane—a part of the other, grown indistinguishable. . . . The pleasure of recognizing a described world is no small thing. (2010: 7)

The happenstance of my trans chest was an eruptive phenomenon that has sutured the links between surgery, theory, and poetics such that I may take pleasure in self-recognition and affirmation. But it is through a sense of being able to feel a way into the poetry of my gender that my greatest pleasure and optimism have rested.

For me, getting my trans chest is like finding extra room for myself. Using the home metaphor— I think of building an extra room. But this notion of structure is complexified by the idea of how one "moves in" to a new room for the self. Berlant's (2004: 450–51) phrase "cultivation of subjectivity" is useful here for theorizing the politics of affect and balancing the "aversive" with the "optimistic." However, I turned to the poetics of affect. My trans chest may be cast richly in the realms of fantasy, or sketchily and peripherally in the hospital clinics, but surgery provides a weird (out of one's own hands), scary moment in which transformation into a different embodied sense happens; a new materiality of touchable, viewable self is made for you. At times, I balked at the reality of surgery; a month before my fifth chest operation, I delayed the date, wanting to articulate my genderqueer, trans-peripheral chest to myself, best of all, in my own poetic conceptualization. It was not only the routinely off-putting clinic effects, the default hospital gender norms, the fear of poor surgical outcomes like infection, or my peripherality to FTM transition that restrained me. I had not yet amalgamated and "homed" my sense of self as I experienced these contingent forces. I still felt rather fearful and clumsy and, to use Crane's term, had not yet succeeded in "transmembering" myself (Doty 2010: 7). I needed to extend my time in creative poetic space, to feel my way into the trans chest I desired. This exposed the importance of allowing for asynchronous timing (institutional time compared with personal time), before giving up to the surgeon's scalpel and the solid erasure of anesthetic unconsciousness.

Doty questions why we should bother with describing the intricacies of the self if such an impulse runs the risk of inaccuracy and clumsiness; his answer is because they are in the "signature of selfhood" (2010: 8). He surmises that "the writer who wants to come closer to the lived texture of experience could do no better than to allow the senses their complexly interactive life" (122). I dilate the meaning of *writer* here to include those genderqueer subjectivities who employ the poetic art of self (also returning to Winterson).

In this article, I have demonstrated something oblique to genderqueer politics—that the cultivation of genderqueer, trans-peripheral poetics in surgical contexts is also a project of genderqueer becoming. Precisely because of the perceptions of not fitting and "not being possible," the experiences of gender trauma require more than "big P" politics. Succor is needed, and a turn to poetics (as a stabilizer for subjectivity and selfhood) offers fruitful conceptual terrain to make the self possible.

My more comfortable queer trans chest may yet rely on the ink of a tattoo artist. My tender and settling scars and my contouring are the newest markers of my physical selfhood. Thinking through the poetics of my chest means describing it to myself (after Doty) in language that matches my feeling of gender. This makes it possible to create and embrace the postsurgical act of tattooing my chest—not using micropigmentation to create three-dimensional-looking nipples but embedding in my skin dotted violet lines and arrows, like those photos archived from my presurgery markings. These will add to the bonus of my surgical happenstance as I am enabled to move beyond and further into the joy of feeling my possible life. This is an intersection of privilege, agency, persistence, luck, and happenstance. Plainly, many folk are not lucky or privileged, and they are rendered invisible and experience ongoing trauma in hospital contexts that they are not supported to resist. What then, should we build from the positive experiences of genderqueer, trans-peripheral, and nonnormatively identifying people in trans surgical settings? My answer to this echoes Winterson, in that inner reality is not "a private hieroglyph" (2008), and while we must acknowledge that gains are being made in Australian general hospitals (the context for my experiences), where staff seek better training to treat and care for a range of gender- and sexually diverse clients, further lines of analysis might examine the value that poetics has more specifically to analyses of crisis. Staying within my local context, I look to contexts of mental health care and other medical settings where agency is routinely and markedly compromised. In this respect, there is much work to do in Australia, where suicidal life, for example, lacks first-person narration and occurs at disproportionately high levels in marginalized socio-cultural contexts.

J. Horncastle is an academic, poet, and writer. They have been teaching and researching in the humanities in Australia since 2005. Their scholarly work draws on existential crisis and the ethics of selfhood and care. An article, "Practicing Care: Queer Vulnerability in the Hospital," was recently published in *Social Identities*.

Notes

1.   I point out that thinking of breast cancer care as if it is "for women" employs a doubly reductive dictum—erroneously implying breast cancer care is exclusive to women, and that "women" are a discrete category of beings. It is expressly noted that *anyone* who has mammary gland tissue has the potential to develop breast cancer and that people who fall outside the normative "woman" category are often marginalized in popular breast cancer discourse.

2.   I endeavor not to make naive or universalizing claims. I write from within an Australian-specific multilayered culture in which Anglo-European discourses of the other are hegemonic. (This especially applies to Australian Indigenous, refugee, queer, disabled, non-Western migrant, asylum seeker, and trans lives that are othered in racist, ableist, or xenophobic senses.) I am critical of this hegemony and aware of my own intersections of privilege and underprivilege amassing within it. To state the obvious, we all have a mixture of diverse life experiences, but this is a facile aspect of homogeneity, and there are hierarchies and oppressions and there are values on coherent identity. While I cannot be apart from the status quo, as if existing outside it as a sovereign autonomous entity, I resist, fighting gender oppression and trans discrimination (for example) at every second.

3.   My comparison to a female-to-male transition context is used as a matter of utility to highlight an issue of legibility. For the sake of clarity in making one point about normative and nonnormative gender subject positions, I avoid referring to possible myriad MTF and FTM transition scenarios. My point *may* resonate for people who identify as gender nonnormative and trans-peripheral (in which case my example of one gender-queer female experience could translate across to other subjectivities) but is not designed to assert this as so; rather, it is to consider one way of thinking about trans-peripherality in a surgical context. When used as a tool to think more philosophically about concepts of becoming and genderqueerness, this surgical transperipherality leads us (for reasons I explain in the final section) to the realm of poetics.

4. Elsewhere (Horncastle 2018), I have analyzed agency and hospital care practices in cancer and mental health contexts. This is less trans-surgery specific, but it extends my discussion of hospital clinic settings here. The important work of Jain (2007a, 2007b), Stacey and Bryson (2012), Bryson and Stacey (2013), and Taylor and Bryson (2016) is especially germane to cancer studies.

5. The short YouTube video preview of *Resisterectomy* (Joynt 2012b), a multimedia art installation by Chase Joynt in collaboration with Mary Bryson, documents gender-diverse body narratives in medical settings, including a breast cancer context. This might provide a very practical talking point for looking critically at routinized norms. In training and education contexts, cancer patients, clinicians, nurses, surgeons, and clinic staff might use this video as a resource for gender-consciousness raising and self-reflexive learning (see Joynt 2012a).

6. I note a private comment from one breast oncology surgeon: she said that her assumptions about breast removal for a heterosexual, cis-male patient with breast cancer were that he would not care about scars and chest aesthetics. In fact the patient complained at her gender normativity and this nudged some progressive thinking for herself, beyond the female- and feminine-breasted model. Likewise, in a conversation with an FTM-identified friend who did not want a mastectomy because he loves and wants to keep his breasts, he was able to easily explain to me that he saw no incoherence with being a breasted man while others (such as medical gatekeepers) were actively resistant to his sense of embodied self. Note that both these examples require the patient to be a hypercognitive, articulate teacher.

7. My use of Butler here does not signal a support for what some trans writers have called a fetishization of violence; for a recent example, see Thom Kai Cheng (in Siemsen 2017). My emphasis on subjectivities that may be subversive and do experience violence does not focus on identity politics or exclude an awareness of the mundane and quotidian. In this article I speak of the "freedom to be," but I am speaking of trans and genderqueer lives in relation to crisis-inducing medical clinics. Actual failure of self as I have indicated above is distinct from living through violence in real and multiple ways. Rage, durability, passion, pleasure, and a thriving or comfortable sense of self are included in my discussions of becoming, and of feeling one's way into home. I note differentiated axes of temporality and materiality. When I speak of agency, individual autonomy is assumed to be contingent, relative, and compromised by paradigms of privilege. The necessity to know exactly "what" one's self is, compared with "who" (offensive or unnecessary for many), is set apart from the necessity for a freedom for all selves to be possible. See Viviane Namaste (2000) and Jay Prosser (1995, 1998) for critiques of Butler's framing of trans subjectivity, and especially Prosser for the concept of "home."

8. In an Australian context, the phrase "maintain the rage" has specific connections to the history of Australian politics and is resonant in Indigenous activism. See Paul Kelly (2001: 196).

References

Berlant, Lauren. 2004. "Critical Inquiry, Affirmative Culture." *Critical Inquiry* 30, no. 2: 445–51.

———. 2007. "Slow Death (Sovereignty, Obesity, Lateral Agency). *Critical Inquiry* 33, no. 4: 754–80.

Beyer, Tamiko. 2012. "Unbordering Bodies." *Glitter Tongue* (blog), February 14. glittertongue .wordpress.com/beyerunbordering-bodies/.

Butler, Judith. 1993. *Bodies That Matter: On the Discursive Limits of Sex*. New York: Routledge.

———. 2004. *Undoing Gender*. New York: Routledge.

Brushwood Rose, Chloe, and Anna Camilleri. 2002. *Brazen Femme: Queering Femininity.* Vancouver: Arsenal Pulp.

Bryson, Mary K., and Jackie Stacey. 2013. "Cancer Knowledge in the Plural: Queering the Biopolitics of Narrative and Affective Mobilities." *Journal of the Medical Humanities* 34, no. 1: 197–212.

Campo, Rafael. 1997. *The Desire to Heal: A Doctor's Education in Empathy, Identity, and Poetry.* London: W. W. Norton.

———. 1999. *Diva.* Durham, NC: Duke University Press.

Carson, Anne. 2006. *Decreation: Poetry, Essays, Opera.* New York: Vintage.

Clare, Eli. 1999. *Exile and Pride: Disability, Queerness, and Liberation.* Cambridge, MA: South End.

———. 2003. "Gawking, Gaping, Staring." *GLQ* 9, nos. 1–2: 257–61.

Creet, Julia. 1991. "Daughter of the Movement: The Psychodynamics of Lesbian S/M Fantasy." *differences* 3, no. 2: 135–59.

Cvetkovich, Ann. 1995. "Sexual Trauma/Queer Memory: Incest, Lesbianism, and Therapeutic Culture." *GLQ* 2, no. 4: 351–77.

Dawn, Amber. 2013. *How Poetry Saved My Life: A Hustler's Memoir.* Vancouver, BC: Arsenal Pulp.

Doty, Mark. 2010. *The Art of Description: World into Word.* Minneapolis: Graywolf.

Duggan, Lisa, and Kathleen McHugh. 1996. "A Fem(me)inist Manifesto." *Women and Performance: A Journal of Feminist Theory* 8, no. 2: 153–59.

Duke University Press. 2017. "Most Read Articles of 2017." Duke University Press blog, December 19. dukeupress.wordpress.com/2017/12/19/the-most-read-articles-of-2017/.

edwards, kari. 2013. "This leftover disruption thing." In *Troubling the Line: Trans and Genderqueer Poetry and Poetics,* edited by T. C. Tolbert and Tim Trace Peterson, 321–25. Callicoon, NY: Nightboat Books.

Eliot, T. S. (1943) 1971. *Four Quartets.* New York: Harvest.

Fisher, Gary. 1996. *Gary in Your Pocket: Stories and Notebooks of Gary Fisher.* Edited by Eve Kosofsky Sedgwick. Durham, NC: Duke University Press.

Fitzal, Florian, and Peter Schrenk, eds. 2015. *Oncoplastic Breast Surgery: A Guide to Clinical Practice.* Vienna: Springer.

Halberstam, Judith. 1998. *Female Masculinity.* Durham, NC: Duke University Press.

Hollibaugh, Amber L. 2000. *My Dangerous Desires: A Queer Girl Dreaming Her Way Home.* Durham, NC: Duke University Press.

Horncastle, J. 2018. "Practicing Care: Queer Vulnerability in the Hospital." *Social Identities: Journal for the Study of Race, Nation and Culture* 24, no. 3: 383–94.

Jain, S. Lochlann. 2007a. "Living in Prognosis: Towards an Elegiac Politics." *Representations* 98, no. 1: 77–92. doi.org/10.1525/rep.2007.98.1.77.

———. 2007b. "Cancer Butch." *Cultural Anthropology* 22, no. 4: 501–38.

Joynt, Chase. 2012a. *Resisterectomy* (Preview). YouTube video, 8:35, posted August 31. www.youtube.com/watch?v=nPLdJMmoTPA.

———. 2012b. *Resisterectomy.* Chase Joynt. chasejoynt.com/projects/resisterectomy/.

Kelly, Paul. 2001. *One Hundred Years: The Australian Story.* Crows Nest, NSW: Allen and Unwin.

Lorde, Audre. 1980. *The Cancer Journals.* San Francisco: Aunt Lute Books.

———. 1981. "An Interview with Audre Lorde." By Adrienne Rich. *Signs* 6, no. 4: 713–36.

———. 1984. *Sister Outsider: Essays and Speeches.* Trumansburg, NY: Crossing.

Macdonald, Joe. 2013. "An Autoethnography of Queer Transmasculine Femme Incoherence and the Ethics of Trans Research." In *Fortieth Anniversary of Studies in Symbolic Interaction,* edited by Norman K. Denzin, 129–52. Bingley, UK: Emerald Group.

McNamara, Jacks. 2013. *Inbetweenland*. Oakland, CA: Deviant Type.

McRuer, Robert. 1997. *The Queer Renaissance: Contemporary American Literature and the Reinvention of Lesbian and Gay Identities*. New York: New York University Press.

———. 2003. "As Good as It Gets: Queer Theory and Critical Disability." *GLQ* 9, nos. 1–2: 79–105.

———. 2006. *Crip Theory: Cultural Signs of Queerness and Disability*. New York: New York University Press.

Muñoz, José E. 2009. *Cruising Utopia: The Then and There of Queer Futurity*. New York: New York University Press.

Namaste, Viviane. 2000. *Invisible Lives: The Erasure of Transsexual and Transgendered People*. Chicago: University of Chicago Press.

Nestle, Joan. 1987. *A Restricted Country*. New York: Firebrand Books.

———. 1998. *A Fragile Union*. San Francisco: Cleis.

Ng, Sally K., et al. 2016. "Breast Reconstruction Post Mastectomy: Patient Satisfaction and Decision Making." *Annals of Plastic Surgery* 76, no. 6: 640–44.

Noble, Bobby J. 2006. *Sons of the Movement: FtMs Risking Incoherence on a Post-queer Cultural Landscape*. Toronto: Women's Press of Canada.

Nordmarken, Sonny. 2014. "Becoming Ever More Monstrous: Feeling Transgender In-Betweenness." *Qualitative Inquiry* 20, no. 1: 37–50.

Piepzna-Samarasinha, Leah Lakshmi. 2015. *Bodymap: Poems*. Toronto: Mawenzi House.

Prosser, Jay. 1995. "No Place Like Home: The Transgendered Narrative of Leslie Feinberg's Stone Butch Blues." *Modern Fiction Studies* 41, no. 3: 483–514.

———. 1998. *Second Skins: The Body Narratives of Transsexuality*. New York: Columbia University Press.

Sandhal, Carrie. 2003. "Queering the Crip or Cripping the Queer? Intersections of Queer and Crip Identities in Solo Autobiographical Performance." *GLQ* 9, nos. 1–2: 25–56.

Sedgwick, Eve K. 1993. *Tendencies*. London: Routledge.

Siemsen, Thora. 2017. "The Rumpus Mini-Interview Project #87: Kai Cheng Thom." *Rumpus*, June 8. therumpus.net/2017/06/the-rumpus-mini-interview-project-87-kai-cheng-thom/.

Spandler, Helen, and Meg-John Barker. 2016. "Mad and Queer Studies: Interconnections and Tensions." *Mad Studies Network* (blog), July 1. madstudies2014.wordpress.com/2016/07/01/mad-and-queer-studies-interconnections-and-tensions/.

Stacey, Jackie, and Mary Bryson. 2012. "Queering the Temporality of Cancer Survivorship." *Aporia* 4, no. 1: 5–17.

Stryker, Susan. 1994. "My Words to Victor Frankenstein above the Village of Chamounix: Performing Transgender Rage." *GLQ* 1, no. 3: 237–54.

Taylor, Evan T., and Mary K. Bryson. 2016. "Cancer's Margins: Trans* and Gender Nonconforming People's Access to Knowledge, Experiences of Cancer Health, and Decision-Making." *LGBT Health* 3, no.1: 79–89. doi.org/10.1089/lgbt.2015.0096.

Volcano, Del LaGrace, and Ulrika Dahl. 2008. *Femmes of Power: Exploding Queer Femininities*. London: Serpent's Tail.

Warner, Michael, ed. 1993. *Fear of a Queer Planet: Queer Politics and Social Theory*. Minneapolis: University of Minnesota Press.

———. 1999. *The Trouble with Normal: Sex, Politics, and the Ethics of Queer Life*. Cambridge, MA: Harvard University Press.

Winterson, Jeanette. 2008. "Shafts of Sunlight." *Guardian*, November 15. www.theguardian.com/books/2008/nov/15/ts-eliot-festival-donmar-jeanette-winterson.

Material Enactments

The Transformational Aesthetics of Cassils and Yishay Garbasz

JULIA STEINMETZ

Abstract Artists Cassils and Yishay Garbasz offer up a series of material enactments on and through the body that articulate a transformational aesthetics of trans subjectivity, one less concerned with representation than with actions and their indexical impacts. Both artists seek out, create, and become transformational objects for the alteration of self-experience. In so doing, each stretches and exceeds the limits of the identitarian, holding together the complexities of conflict and leaving room for the work of the unconscious in expansive imaginings of what it is to act as an artist in the sphere of the political while inhabiting the messy materiality of the body in the world. As viewers, we are drawn into complex dynamics of enacting the desires and fantasies of the psyche on, in, and through the materiality of the flesh.
Keywords transformation, aesthetics, materiality

E leanor Antin's *Carving: A Traditional Sculpture* was created for the 1972 Whitney Biennial, which at the time had no category for performance art: all entries had to be designated as painting, drawing, photography, or sculpture. Antin cheekily entered her performance documentation, which took the form of photographs, and titled the work a "traditional sculpture." This title referenced formal changes in her own body enacted via a crash diet and purposely toyed with the traditional process of classical sculptors, who were said to find their ideal form by chipping away at a block of marble and discarding any unnecessary material. Antin's time-lapse performance of whittling down her nude body to "make an academic sculpture" functioned as a feminist critique of the social pressure to make bodies conform to an aesthetic, binary-gendered cultural ideal. Cassils's performance *Cuts: A Traditional Sculpture* (2011) signifies beyond the artist's striking invocation of Antin's *Carving*. The artist's body is a sculptural index of disciplined practices: as opposed to Antin's mechanism of carving/starving, which is an actively passive withholding and refusal, Cassils's cuts are precise and

TSQ: Transgender Studies Quarterly ★ Volume 5, Number 2 ★ May 2018
DOI 10.1215/23289252-4348696 © 2018 Duke University Press

technical, mobilizing intense physical labor and a frenzy of consumption bordering on the abject. These cuts are designed to pointedly elide the surgeon's knife in the production of a decidedly beefcake transmasculine form. The artist's decision to take (illegal) steroids for the final eight weeks of the project enacts a modulation of the endocrine system, which when combined with intense physical training and massive caloric intake facilitated transformation into a muscle-bound "cut" physique without the use of testosterone or traditional surgical intervention. *Cuts* includes captivating yet revolting time-lapse imagery and slow-motion takes of the artist eating raw meat with animalistic fervor, swallowing raw eggs, and choking on a face full of pills. What we are seeing is a profound act of consumption combined with the almost orgasmic exertion of "maxing out" in pursuit of a bodily image that is ultimately unsustainable, a perpetual self-fashioning with fleeting moments of fruition captured by the artist's photographs and rosy watercolor renditions.

Cassils's reinterpretation of Antin's *Carving* was initially conceived for an exhibition at LACE (Los Angeles Contemporary Exhibitions) that staged an exploration of relationships between feminist generations. Cassils exhibited *Cuts* alongside their take on another classic of 1970s feminist body art: Lynda Benglis's *Advertisement*. By her own account, Benglis wanted more playfulness with gender roles and sexually explicit imagery than the women's movement offered up. Antin created a pinup-style portrait of herself wearing only sunglasses and a double-ended dildo, which functioned as a centerfold when printed as an advertisement in *Artforum Magazine*. Less of a straight critique than Antin's piece, Benglis's "dildo ad" was seen by many as an attack on feminism rather than a manifestation of it. To *Artforum*'s associate editors, for example, the Benglis spread constituted "a shabby mockery of the aims" of the movement for women's liberation, while to feminist critic Cindy Nemser it was "in the end . . . another means of manipulating men through the exploitation of female sexuality" (1975: 7). Though Benglis's work was dismissed at the time, the image holds a sexual lawlessness and graphic immediacy that was also a radical confrontation with both art and feminism in 1974. Both works provoke relevant and complex observations about a woman's place within the art world and society and as well address objectification and commoditization of the female body.

Cassils commented on the preparation of reinterpretations of these feminist classics, saying, "Rather than starve myself like Antin I will be building my body, and unlike Benglis's ad, whose body is seen as sexy and salacious, my body will be an abject and confounding body, not a socially acceptable body. These new interpretations will cause a rupture in the mind of the viewer, bringing forth the history of feminist discussion but also pushing it further" (LACE 2011). By reenacting the formal tropes of these works, Cassils manifests their own desire to place a queerly sculpted body within the frame of these historical and iconic

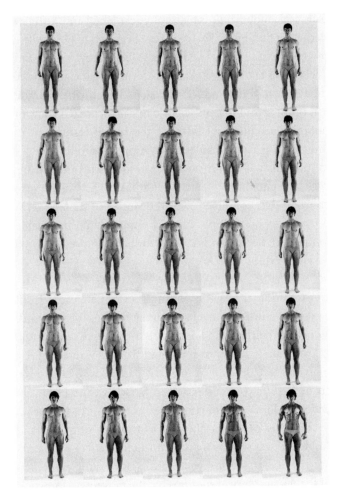

Figure 1. Cassils, *Cuts: A Traditional Sculpture*, time lapse (front), 2017. Courtesy Ronald Feldman Fine Arts

performance documents. *Advertisement: Hommage to Benglis* features the artist's muscular physique photographed in collaboration with Robin Black, at the peak of a 160-day durational performance, using flesh as sculptural material. While Benglis's original *Advertisement* acted as a commentary on sexist gender-based limitations in the art world, Cassils's *Hommage* uses the same strategies to intervene in the gendered policing of trans and nonconforming bodies in the world at large. If performativity is a "saying something" that *does* something, then enactment is a "doing something" that *says* something. Operating at the intersection of performance, sculpture, and photography, Cassils uses a mastery of techniques of the body to achieve desired performative and sculptural effects. In processes laden with exhaustion, pain, nausea, *jouissance*, and trembling, Cassils draws us into the

Figure 2. Yishay Garbasz, *Eat Me Damien*, 2010. Formaldehyde protected testicles removed during surgery. Courtesy Ronald Feldman Fine Arts

intense emotional valence of enacting the desires and fantasies of the psyche on, in, and through the materiality of the flesh.

Michelangelo famously described his approach to sculpture as one of liberating the figure from the material that imprisons it. We see this liberatory approach most clearly in his intentionally unfinished *Slaves*, which in their incompletion render the process of cutting and carving that coaxes the figurative form from the stone. The indexical traces of the sculptor's knife and chisel make the artist's labor visible, even as it reveals the musculature of the body of the slave, itself formed by labor in perpetuity, incompletely liberated, *non-finito*. This formal structure, foregrounding the materiality of the body and the labor through which it is made and remade, is the armature on which the sculptural body art of both Cassils and British-Israeli artist Yishay Garbasz rests. Both artists are represented by Ronald Feldman Fine Arts in New York City, which resulted in their work being exhibited together in the gallery's group show *Have We Met Before?* This curatorial pairing placed Cassils's *Cuts* alongside Garbasz's *Becoming* (2010) and *Eat Me, Damien*, offering up a series of material enactments on and through the body that articulate a transformational aesthetics of trans subjectivity, one less concerned with representation than with actions and their indexical impacts.

Garbasz is an artist who performs photographic enactments via excursions into deeply contested landscape. Her recent work presents performative photographic and sculptural elements born of her travels to Belfast, the West Bank, and the Northern Limit Line separating North and South Korea. Electrified razor wire installed in the gallery and photographs of the literal barriers separating warring factions living in close proximity form the explicit content of the work, which was brought together in Garbasz's 2015 solo exhibition *Severed Connections: Do What I Say or They Will Kill You*, presented at Ronald Feldman Fine Arts. Garbasz photographs with a large-format camera, lugging a mass of gear through treacherous terrain. These photographs of the razor wire and minefields of the Northern Limit Line and the bombed-out territories of the West Bank are a double-pointed index—they evidence both the landscape in front of the lens and the body of the artist behind it. The conditions of the work's possibility lie in the wagers the artist enacts between risk and representation. This enactment of bodily vulnerability plays out perhaps most dramatically in the artist's series of images shot in the Fukushima Nuclear Exclusion Zone, the subject of her 2014 solo exhibition *Ritual and Reality*. The artist captured abandoned houses and cars, empty hospitals, and strangely serene spaces of leisure such as driving ranges alongside fields of nuclear waste storage and guarded checkpoints sectioning off the radioactive exclusion zone. In a series of ten-minute videos that are nearly static under the hush of evacuation, the tick of the Geiger counter monitoring Garbasz's exposure to radiation in the course of making the images is a haunting soundtrack.

This commitment to traveling to the site of atrocities can be traced back to Garbasz's earlier, more autobiographical work. The artist's 2009 photographic book *In My Mother's Footsteps* retraced every location her mother inhabited and traveled through as a child in Nazi Germany, in exile in the Netherlands, and as a prisoner in the work and death camps of Westerbork, Terezin, Auschwitz, Christianstadt, and Bergen-Belsen, which she survived. Garbasz writes, "I feel that my mother lost parts of her soul in those places. I felt that I had to go back and collect them" (2009: 7). The process of retracing her mother's steps and making this photographic journey took a year, and it profoundly impacted Garbasz's mother, who was able to see the images before she died. Home may be where we start from, but it is only the beginning of the arc toward the location of cultural experience, the place where the performativity of performance does its work. *In My Mother's Footsteps* is forged in an intermediate zone between finding and creating, by means of a process that psychoanalyst Christopher Bollas (1987: 40) describes as "transformational object-seeking": "Transformational object-seeking is an endless memorial search for something in the future that resides in the past. I believe that if we investigate the many types of object relating, we will discover that the subject is seeking the transformational object and aspiring to be matched in symbiotic harmony within an aesthetic frame that promises to metamorphose the self." In the wake of this journey into her mother's past, Garbasz undertook *The Numbers Project*, in which she branded herself with her mother's identification number from the Nazi camps. Documentation of this action was exhibited alongside the artist's *Becoming* project, which captured her gender transition via self-portraits made into a zoetrope, and the performative sculpture *Eat Me Damian*, which consists of Garbasz's testicles floating in a tank of formaldehyde. While *Becoming*, like Cassils's *Cuts*, references the durational body-art aesthetics of Antin's *Carving*, *Eat Me Damien* treats the artist's body parts as a ready-made. Using the signature sculptural technique of Damien Hirst, famously debuted with the display of a tiger shark preserved in a formaldehyde solution in his 1991 *The Physical Impossibility of Death in the Mind of the Living*, Garbasz uses the by-products of her gender-confirmation surgery as another kind of specimen. This sculpture deploys a very particular kind of performativity: it presents the viewer with the kind of evidence often demanded by the transphobic and trans-curious, radically foreclosing the genre of questions epitomized by "what's between your legs?" It also acts as a pointed critique of the masculinist aesthetics and capitalist market-driven ethos Hirst embodies, as well as the practices of classification, taxonomy, and display endemic to both the natural history museum and the medico-legal complex.

The body of work presented by Cassils and Garbasz is defined by action; one might be tempted to call it "acting out" or perhaps more aptly "acting up." With this in mind, it becomes evident that the work of these two artists requires a critical framework organized not only by performance and performativity but also by enactment. Both artists seek out, create, and become transformational objects for the alteration of self-experience; in so doing, each stretches and exceeds the limits of the identitarian, holding together the complexities of conflict and leaving room for the work of the unconscious in expansive imaginings of what it is to act as an artist in the sphere of the political while inhabiting the messy materiality of the body in the world.

Julia Steinmetz is a performance studies scholar, contemporary art writer, visual artist, and performer. She is currently a visiting assistant professor in the Performance and Performance Studies MFA Program at Pratt Institute in Brooklyn, New York. She holds a PhD in performance studies and an MFA in photography and media. Her work has appeared in *Signs*, *GSQ*, *E-misférica*, and *Women and Performance*, as well as the edited volumes *Queer* (2016) and *Commerce by Artists* (2011). She coedited the "Feminist Landscapes" special issue of *Women and Performance* with Katherine Brewer-Ball. Her book manuscript "Here and Now: Relational Psychoanalysis and the Transformational Aesthetics of Contemporary Performance" focuses on mechanisms of psychic, interpersonal, and social transformation in the scene of aesthetic encounter.

References

Bollas, Christopher. 1987. *The Shadow of the Object: Psychoanalysis of the Unthought Known.* New York: Columbia University Press.

Cassils. 2011. *Cuts: A Traditional Sculpture.* Exhibition catalogue. New York: Ronald Feldman Fine Arts.

Garbasz, Yishay. 2009. *In My Mother's Footsteps.* Ostfildern, Germany: Hatje Cantz.

———. 2010. *Becoming: A Gender Flipbook.* New York: Mark Batty.

LACE (Los Angeles Contemporary Exhibitions). 2011. *LACE Live!* Exhibition press release, September.

Nemser, Cindy. 1975. "Lynda Benglis: A Case of Sexual Nostalgia." *Feminist Art Journal,* Winter, 74–75.

"Am I Gonna Become Famous When I Get My Boobs Done?"

Surgery and Celebrity in Gigi Gorgeous: This Is Everything

DAN UDY

Abstract *Gigi Gorgeous: This Is Everything* (dir. Barbara Kopple, 2017) is a feature-length documentary following the life of Canadian YouTube video blogger Giselle "Gigi" Lazzarato—aka Gigi Gorgeous—currently distributed on the site's premium streaming feature, YouTube Red. As one of YouTube's most high-profile content producers and its most successful trans video blogger ("vlogger"), Lazzarato has thoroughly documented her life on-screen; however, she has largely avoided sharing details of her surgical procedures. *This Is Everything* takes a closer look at her rise to fame alongside the story of her gender transition, revealing how Lazzarato has carefully engineered the documentation of her surgeries to navigate the burgeoning marketplace of online celebrity. Following Jasbir K. Puar, this review argues that the film demonstrates an axiomatic case of "piecing" the transgender body that extends the temporality of surgical procedures, thus mapping the rehabilitation of transgender subjects into productive citizens of the neoliberal US economy.
Keywords YouTube, celebrity, documentary, surgery, transgender

At present, Giselle "Gigi" Lazzarato has 2.7 million subscribers to her YouTube channel, "Gigi Gorgeous." Her videos are uploaded every few days and range from glamorous holiday diaries and beauty product promotions to video confessionals and collaborations with other YouTubers. Having begun her career in 2008 recording makeup tutorials from her parents' home in Toronto, Lazzarato quickly gained a large following and substantial income before coming out as transgender and beginning her medical transition. Seven years later, she moved to Los Angeles, California, after starting hormone replacement therapy (HRT) and undergoing a tracheal shave, facial feminization surgery, and breast augmentation.[1] She is now the highest-earning trans video producer on YouTube and represents the most successful exploitation of a DIY media genre identified by scholars such as Avery Dame, Laura Horak, and Tobias Raun: the trans video blog ("vlog"). Lazzarato is often cited by other vloggers as a model of entrepreneurial and surgical success, and her place at the forefront of this genre has been cemented by Barbara Kopple's feature-length documentary *Gigi Gorgeous: This Is Everything* (2017), which maps how her gender transition and entry into the burgeoning marketplace of YouTube celebrity were closely intertwined.[2]

As Dame, Horak, and Raun all note, trans vlogs follow a well-worn set of formal conventions. They are mostly produced by web users in their teens to mid-twenties, consist of talking-head confessionals filmed in domestic interiors, are relatively short (up to twenty minutes in length), and use informal direct address ("Hey guys!") to establish intimacy between speaker and audience (Dame 2013; Horak 2014; Raun 2016). A large subset of vloggers produce retrospective slide-shows that establish a "before" and "after" of medical transition and use chronological markers of hormone treatment in their videos; Horak names this linear temporality "hormone time" and writes that it works toward a future "in which the subject experiences harmony between the felt and perceived body" (2014: 580). She concedes that the formulaic nature of the genre is certainly open to critique but argues that it provides a blueprint that "help[s] amateurs enter the field and attract new viewers" (573). However, online popularity—quantified through views and subscription numbers—is nonetheless guided by Western standards of beauty and gender presentation, and many trans vloggers of color are locked out from the audiences reached by their white counterparts (Horak 2014; Raun 2016). In many respects, Lazzarato follows such tropes to the letter and has benefited hugely from YouTube's racial bias alongside its valorization of youth and physical attractiveness. Yet despite being a figurehead of the genre, she largely avoids the use of "hormone time" and surgical recovery videos on her channel.[3] In fact, she has eschewed documenting her major surgeries and HRT altogether, instead producing talking-head confessionals recounting her procedures only after she has fully healed. What transpires in *This Is Everything*, however, is that Lazzarato secretly filmed herself during her transition and documented her consultations and recoveries as she traveled to and from the United States for surgery. She stored this footage on hard drives that she nicknamed her "vault," in anticipation of a future project possibly beyond the realm of YouTube (Steinmetz 2017). After being approached by director Barbara Kopple, she agreed to hand over the files along with home movies from her childhood, and these were then edited together with preexisting YouTube clips, new interviews, and footage shot after her relocation to Los Angeles in 2015.

With its prototypical "before" shots and intimate recovery footage, *This Is Everything* paradoxically marks Lazzarato's engagement with the tropes of transition vlogs at the moment in which, for the very first time, she relinquishes control of her own story. Kopple begins her documentary in the traditional fashion of mainstream transgender biography, splicing interviews with family members who reflect on how Lazzarato was always "different" between grainy home videos of her subject as a junior competitive diver. Viewers are then guided into Lazzarato's teenage years, in which she narrates her discovery of YouTube over clips from her early makeup tutorials. Her gender-nonconforming presentation and her advice to "always be yourself" chimed with an audience of young people who were using Web 2.0 platforms to connect with others like them; it also caught the attention of makeup brands and other sponsors keen to capitalize on this new mode of media production and consumption. Lazzarato explains, "Coming out as gay made my presence online soar. . . . That's how I met my manager, Scott Fisher," a similarly precocious entrepreneur who spotted his client's videos and began arranging business deals on his Blackberry while working on shift at Starbucks. Under Fisher's guidance, Lazzarato turned her newfound celebrity into a lucrative income and was quickly earning $16,000 a month through advertising deals and event appearances. Although this new phase of her career also included a YouTube scripted reality series—*The Avenue* (2011–13), coproduced by Fisher—Kopple omits this detail from her film.

In February 2012 Lazzarato took a twenty-day break from YouTube following her mother's death from leukemia and brain cancer. In her voice-over interview, she explains how this trauma prompted her to begin medical transition, which she revealed to her viewers in her second coming-out video the following year.[4] Kopple effects "hormone time" by annotating the clip with Lazzarato's age—twenty years old—and links this public announcement to her increasing profile as a role model for queer and trans youth, evidenced by massive queues for meet-and-greets where fans are often driven to tears. This ever-increasing celebrity and its attendant commercial rewards also enable her to self-finance major medical procedures, at which point she starts recording for what would eventually become *This Is Everything*. Her surgery diaries begin after completing one year of HRT, in which she stands topless in her bathroom while applying makeup and reflects on the physical and psychological changes that treatment has, or has not, produced. In the following scene, Lazzarato goes online to show the camera the website of her facial feminization surgeon, Dr. Jeffrey Spiegel, before visiting her father to tell him that she has paid $14,000 and will shortly be traveling to Boston for a chin and forehead reduction. He insists on accompanying her to the surgery alongside friend Tiffany Namtu, who takes charge of camerawork when Lazzarato is unable to film herself; when alone, she sets up her camera in her hotel suite to document the mundane and painful routine of postoperative care, and her dressings indicate that another procedure, a rhinoplasty, was also performed. At home in Toronto two months later, her certificate of name change from the Ontario government arrives in the post. Shortly afterward, she returns to her laptop to plan for her breast augmentation and comes across Beverly Hills surgeon Dr. Stuart Linder, whose website includes vivid graphics of his reality TV credentials. "Am I gonna become famous when I get my boobs done?" she jokingly asks her brother, just out of shot.

During her month long stay in Los Angeles, Lazzarato's father assists with recovery before Namtu and Fisher fly in from Toronto. She is eager to show her friends her new breasts and soon goes shopping for expensive bras with fellow YouTuber Trisha Paytas. Although nudity marks the most immediate difference between her YouTube vlogs and this footage from the "vault," such scenes also possess a comparatively rough aesthetic and unfold at slower speed. Shaky camerawork, awkward framing, low light levels, and shifts in focus all distinguish these clips from the fast edits and careful composition of the videos on her YouTube channel. This disjuncture magnifies the temporal difference between *This Is Everything* and the vlogs from which it draws, but it also disrupts the linear logic of hormone time that Kopple tries her best to instate; although Lazzarato does not appear in interview until after her surgical diaries are complete, millions of web users have already followed her transition online, and for such viewers her physical appearance in Kopple's interviews comes as no surprise. As a result, the film extends the temporality of surgical procedures and, when coupled with Lazzarato's strategic relocation to California, encapsulates what Jasbir K. Puar (2015) terms the neoliberal "piecing" of the transgender body. Kopple's interviews with Lazzarato's team indicate a fierce drive to move their client up the ladder of Hollywood celebrity, suggesting that their staggered release of surgery footage is an integral part of doing so. By placing such clips in the hands of an Oscar-winning filmmaker, they clearly hope to improve Lazzarato's credibility as a businesswoman and potential brand collaborator.

In "Bodies with New Organs: Becoming Trans, Becoming Disabled," Puar writes that "neoliberal mandates regarding productive, capacitated bodies entrain the trans body to recreate an abled body not only in terms of gender and sexuality but also in terms of economic productivity and the economic development of national economy" (2015: 47). This takes place through the act of "piecing," which "is a recruitment into neoliberal forms of fragmentation of the body for capitalist profit" that works by "extending the body experientially and extracting value not just from bodies but from body parts and particles" (47, 54). Although this could be applied to all those who vlog their surgeries, advertising revenue is accessible only for videos with over 100,000 views—few have reached Lazzarato's level of subscribers, and fewer still have negotiated as many alternative streams of income that stretch beyond YouTube itself. Instead, *This Is Everything* demonstrates how Lazzarato's story is the axiomatic example of such "recruitment," consolidated by her move from Canada to the United States. Kopple's contemporary footage begins with her subject driving a customized sports car through the streets of Los Angeles, symbolizing Lazzarato's entry into a group of young, self-made millionaires that make up a rapidly growing segment of the American workforce (we are reminded that, at this point, she is still only twenty-three).

The federal and state taxes Lazzarato now pays build on the revenue already made for YouTube's parent company, Google, which in turn continues to grow as she links her viewers to the pay-walled film at the end of each new vlog. As such, Kopple's documentary magnifies Lazzarato's new position as a productive member of the US economy and extends the extraction of value from her body begun by her earlier vlogs. After her surgeries are complete, her team turns its focus to next steps that might transcend the bounds of YouTube celebrity. They conclude the film by sending their client to New York Fashion Week, before which manager Adam Wescott tells her that "when a brand who wants to hire you as their spokesperson for a very long period of time Googles you, they're gonna see fashion week and that's gonna be more credible than you at freakin' RuPaul's Drag Race premiere." "We have to keep evolving everything we're doing so that it becomes something bigger," he explains. One year later, Revlon Cosmetics announced Lazzarato as its new ambassador the same day that *This Is Everything* premiered online.

Dan Udy is a PhD candidate in the Department of English at King's College London. He has previously published work in *Gender, Place and Culture*, *Jump Cut: A Review of Contemporary Media*, and the edited collection *Unpopular Culture* (2016).

Notes

1. These are the procedures Lazzarato has documented on her YouTube channel and as part of *This Is Everything*. In the film she explains that she will not disclose whether she has undergone gender-confirmation surgery.

2. For example, vlogger Stef Sanjati cites Lazzarato's surgical results as a reason for choosing Dr. Jeffrey Spiegel for her own facial feminization surgery (Sanjati 2017).

3. In her first and only vlog documenting a surgical procedure, Lazzarato recounts her tracheal shave to the camera and shows before and after photographs alongside footage of her traveling to her appointment (Gigi Gorgeous 2014). For her hormone treatment and major surgeries, she did not share any recovery footage or chronological updates, and although she has posted videos documenting laser hair removal and eyebrow tattooing, I categorize these among her beauty vlogs designed for a wider audience, including cisgender women.

4. This video, "I Am Transgender | Gigi," was uploaded in December 2013. Lazzarato has since released a third coming-out video in which she identifies as a lesbian, having begun a relationship with the oil heiress Natalia Getty (Gigi Gorgeous 2013, 2016).

References

Dame, Avery. 2013. "'I'm Your Hero? Like Me?': The Role of 'Expert' in the Trans Male Vlog." *Journal of Language and Sexuality* 2, no. 1: 40–69.

Horak, Laura. 2014. "Trans on YouTube: Intimacy, Visibility, Temporality." *TSQ* 1, no. 4: 572–85.

Puar, Jasbir K. 2015. "Bodies with New Organs: Becoming Trans, Becoming Disabled." *Social Text*, no. 124: 45–73.

Raun, Tobias. 2016. *Out Online: Trans Self-Representation and Community Building on YouTube.* London: Routledge.

Steinmetz, Katy. 2017. "Gigi Gorgeous on Her Documentary: 'It's a Raw Look into My Life.'" *Time*, February 8. time.com/4661698/gigi-gorgeous-documentary-interview/.

Videography

Gigi Gorgeous. 2013. "I Am Transgender | Gigi." YouTube video, 4:08, posted December 16. www.youtube.com/watch?v=srOsrIC9Gj8.

———. 2014. "My Plastic Surgery Experience | Gigi." YouTube video, 8:20, posted March 3. www.youtube.com/watch?v=jSLGrHtiH78.

———. 2016. "I'm a Lesbian | Gigi." YouTube video, 8:28, posted September 14. www.youtube.com/watch?v=4HclVrFsAnY.

Sanjati, Stef. 2017. "My Facial Reconstruction | Stef Sanjati." YouTube video, 29:04, posted February 13. www.youtube.com/watch?v=PqNkzpZEfj4.

Interview with Blogger/Vlogger FinnTheInficible

"People Don't Like Making Themselves Public for Having Phalloplasty"

TOBIAS RAUN

Abstract *TSQ*'s "New Media" section editor Tobias Raun interviews the British blogger/vlogger FinnTheInficible, who has been very open online about the physical and emotional process of having phalloplasty. He started video blogging in 2012, when he came out as trans on YouTube. His social media presence has since then increased and spread across media platforms (YouTube, Tumblr, Instagram, Facebook, Twitter, etc.). In this interview, Raun and FinnTheInficible discuss issues such as sensitivity and empowerment in relation to the public sharing of personal experiences with having phalloplasty. As argued by FinnTheInficible, more information is still needed on phalloplasty as well as improved communication between health-care professionals and trans people, not least to improve the aftercare.
Keywords blog, vlog, FinnTheInficible, phalloplasty

As a researcher, I have been studying transgender self-representation and community building online since 2009, trying to unfold the practices and cultures thriving here as well as the potentials and challenges of sidestepping the traditional media channels (e.g., Raun 2012, 2015b, 2016a, 2016b; Raun and Keegan 2017). Transgender knowledge sharing was changed with the advent of platforms like YouTube, which offered a multimodal opportunity to document and discuss—among other things—transitioning technologies and processes. Closed, primarily text-based forums were supplemented by a site that was public, hence easily accessible, and where audio-visuality played a key role as *the* prime source of knowledge production. With YouTube one could actually *hear* and *see* what transitioning technologies enable and what it felt like to go through these transitioning processes. Knowledge about and visualizations of the effects of hormones and surgeries were no longer exclusively the property of the medical

TSQ: Transgender Studies Quarterly ★ Volume 5, Number 2 ★ May 2018 **281**
DOI 10.1215/23289252-4348722   © 2018 Duke University Press

establishment but were made publicly available, challenging existing hierarchies of voice and agency. Transgender people literally became more visible to self and others. Transgender men documented "the wonders of testosterone" at length and with a frequency that counteracted how these processes had previously been shrouded in mystery (Raun 2015a). Likewise, top surgery became a commonly occurring topic as numerous trans men appeared bare chested, offering advice on how to sculpt and care for the surgically altered chest. However, extensive information on and representations of bottom surgery for trans men were absent. Firsthand experiences of phalloplasty and metoidioplasty were for a very long time nonexistent. For trans women this was different. Here footage from recovery rooms was present alongside extensive information on the process and procedure of vaginoplasty and labiaplasty. One was often left with the feeling that trans men did not pursue such surgeries and/or that the results were too bad and therefore not worth talking about in public. Or as stated in the ground-breaking book *Hung Jury: Testimonies of Genital Surgery by Transsexual Men*, information tended to be absent, false, or misleading, perpetuating "the myth that FTM genital surgery is unsuccessful and produces aesthetically poor, non-functioning penises" (Cotten 2012: 3). But recently things have started to change with bloggers/vloggers like FinnTheInficible, who is one of the pioneers on YouTube in breaking the silence and secrecy around bottom surgery for trans men. I interviewed FinnTheInficible about his motivations and concerns about speaking in public about his own experiences with having phalloplasty.

Tobias: *You share a lot about both the physical aspects of lower surgery and the emotional aspects—why did you decide to do that?*

Finn: I tend to talk about the emotional stuff on YouTube (2017a) and the physical stuff on my Tumblr (2017b), but of course they do cross over. It was a really hard decision to decide to talk about phalloplasty on my channel, one that I still struggle with because top surgery is one thing, but genitals it's another. . . . I would never ever show my bits on YouTube, never. I know that there are people who do that, but I would never ever do that—it's my boundary, there is no way that happens. But for me, when I was trying to work out if I wanted phalloplasty, there was nothing, absolutely so little out there. And the people that I managed to get in touch with and that helped me, I just really feel that I want to pay that forward and give some information to people out there. When it comes to me in relation to YouTube, I do talk about it, but I try to keep it more to how I feel now that I'm having the surgery, and what the process *feels like*, and when you need pictures and real intimate discussion, that goes on my Tumblr. If I am going to talk about something really intimately, I do say look if you don't want to hear this put your hands over your ears, trigger warnings. But yeah, it's a difficult one.

Tobias: *You are present on many social media platforms—what are your criteria for what you share where?*

Finn: I think it is about boundaries. Because in the beginning I was very out there on YouTube, and people could follow me on Facebook and all of that, but I cut that off because I'd like to keep my personal Facebook just for me just to give me a little space. I set up a Facebook page [a fan page; see Finn 2017c] to run alongside my YouTube channel so that people could then come through my YouTube space to connect with me there but still give me my own private space. With Facebook you can't really put anything graphic on there anyway, Tumblr—no rules—you can put whatever on Tumblr! So I chose Tumblr for that reason. And also it gives you the option of, at the end of a post, to read more, and then you can have the photos on that bit. Now, many haven't got a clue how to do that, so you really have to look for the photos so that hopefully only people who really want to see results or are interested come. On my WordPress [Finn 2017d] I would never post pictures of myself there because you can't hide them as successfully on there. Well, I know that they are not completely hidden on Tumblr, but you need to work to find them.

Tobias: *So you perceive Tumblr as a different kind of platform?*

Finn: Yes! . . . It's kind of more relaxed. My WordPress, because I am writing as well, it's more like my professional kind of place [*makes air quotes*]. . . . It [phalloplasty] just doesn't feel as if it belongs on WordPress. I am presenting myself as a writer, but you can actually get a link to my Tumblr on my WordPress. But to me it felt like I needed to separate the two off. And also, at some point I might shut my Tumblr, I don't know.

Tobias: *You said that there wasn't much information out there on phalloplasty when you started looking yourself. Where did you look?*

Finn: My God, I looked everywhere! People don't like making themselves public for having phalloplasty. So you really got to dig. So I talked to somebody, and then they'd say try this Tumblr account, and it was just word of mouth in the end so that I managed to get a bit more information. In the last year or two—there are loads of people blogging about it now, but there weren't back then. There were a lot of Yahoo groups that I was directed to, but I found them quite useless in the end. . . . You see, people don't put the sources out there because it's so delicate, isn't it? You really got to want to have phalloplasty to have them. So it is so hard to access these things. And there is such a lot of misinformation out there, which was another reason why I did this. Because I had been somebody who talked about lower surgery without really having looked at it. . . . But once dysphoria increased, then I started to look and persevered more, but that's what it is—you have to persevere to find the good stuff, and I do find that's still the case, it takes persevering to find it. . . . After first getting rid of all the awful results [in the Yahoo groups], I found loads of files of people who had amazing results—"wow okay, this is actually something that is achievable and long-winded." I spoke to people who had awful complications but yet were still very happy and would not change it because of the end results, and that's what changed my mind. Okay, the realistic thing is, this *is* hard work, this *is* painful, all of that, but most of the time now you end up lying with a functioning penis you're happy with, so that's what did it for me in the end. . . . I also read *Hung Jury* and that changed my mind—about everything, really. Because there is so much bad information out there, and a lot of people were quite anti–lower surgery for a while, and I also was of the mindset "I don't need a penis," and then I changed my mind and wanted to be really honest about why that was and what really happened. Because I really like the idea—and I still believe it—you don't need a penis to be a man, it's not in your genitals, it's in yourself. Some need testosterone and some don't. Some need surgery and some don't. And I really wanted to get that across and then suddenly I go, "ohhhhh actually I'm having surgery," it was just like, "wow okay." I wanted to share why that was. Because I was subject to loads of . . . misinformation.

Tobias: *Did you feel like you had to justify it?*

Finn: A little, yeah, because I was really like . . . Buck Angel was my hero, that he could live and deal with what was downstairs and be happy, and I wanted to be like that. I really did. And I didn't want to go through lower surgery, and the lower surgery I had seen was awful. And I realize now that I had not seen complete results, so I kind of made all of these assumptions. No, I'm gonna be a man without a penis and I'm going to be proud of it. So to go like, no I've changed my mind was quite hard. So not justify as such but just explain that it is okay to have a penis but equally it's okay to realize that you misread things and this is what you want.

Tobias: *Do you feel that there is more knowledge sharing now back and forth between the medical establishment and trans experiences in regard to phalloplasty?*

Finn: [*Shakes his head*] We are left in the dark! It is SO SO hard. It's another reason why I share because they do our surgeries and then they go "bye bye," and then we are left to kind of like fend for ourselves. And I don't think that half the time they really know what's going on themselves. I only found out this recently that—because there [are] no statistics, well there are few statistics on any of this—with ureteral hookup, which I knew was the hardest part, I had my last issue, and they said at the end of the day we don't know long-term results of what happens to men because we don't have any long-term studies, so they don't actually tell us this. It seems to be a lot of them holding back, so you got the medical pressure on one side and the other going, "we need more information," but I don't know why they are not more forthcoming with it, I really don't. So it's the blind leading the blind half the time and it's dangerous. Because actually the results now are SO SO good, my concern is, if we are not being told properly how to take care of ourselves after surgery, then we can actually end up messing up the results. You need the surgeon to communicate more honestly, but they just don't.

Tobias: *Why do you think that is?*

Finn: I don't think they understand. I think they understand the physical aspect in terms of what goes where, but I think in terms of what it is to be transgender and how that feels I don't think they got a clue. . . . I don't think they understand the full implication of what it is to have this dysphoria, I don't think they get it. So as far as they are concerned, "we're the surgeons, we have the power, we've done the surgery, we know what we are talking about, now you go home." It's just not good enough actually. But you don't want to complain because there are only three surgeons who do this in our country [the United Kingdom], so we can't go anywhere else, so it's this stalemate where you dare not say anything for fear of having this surgery taken away. It's worrying, really worrying.

Tobias: *Do you think the surgeons or doctors know enough of this aftercare?*

Finn: Probably not. I don't know how they are even learning about it. We come home and see our local GP [general practitioner] for it. And other than a brief letter between the two, they know nothing. So there is a big gap actually. They could do a lot better by working more closely together. . . . I'm very good, I e-mail pictures to them constantly, I properly annoy the hell out of them! I e-mail all my pictures because I need to be told "is this okay, does this look okay?" I take charge of my own healing. But that's an issue with this, that's why I share about this, you have to take responsibility for your side of the healing, that should be the case, now I agree with that, but if you don't you're stuck, so you need to be proactive and e-mail them and harass them and go: "look I need this wound looked at, I want to be told if it's okay." You know with any other surgery you'd have a real line of follow-up but there isn't . . . and there is no connection back, and I think that's dangerous for people that aren't really proactive, and that's half the point of why I share and say "hey look, you've had this surgery, make sure you take charge, make sure you put stuff in place."

Tobias: *Aside from wanting to put more information out there and share it with other people, are you also using your own blogging and vlogging practice to find people to share knowledge with about your own process?*

Finn: Yeah, we are amazing in our community sharing with each other [about] surgery and what's happened. But what I also hope for my YouTube is that surgeon consultants might see it. I really do hope that by putting it out there this is what is happening. Because I actually feel very protective about the phalloplasty procedure. Because I was so anti it, because of the wrong information I had of it, I now realize it can be very successful, it can be aesthetically pleasing, functional—all of these things, but I was told it wasn't, so I feel very protective. If we are not given the right aftercare, surgeries can go wrong and badly affect the statistics and people can recourse all this misinformation about things. I don't think it's the phalloplasty that's got the issue now, but it's the aftercare, the lack of communication that cause[s] it. I also share because, look, it *is* really good results, and what breaks down is the aftercare communication. Because I don't want it to get a bad reputation by them not doing their job properly. If you've watched my videos, you know how much they stuffed me over royally really, really badly, and I want to complain but I dare not so instead I share about it very balanced on my YouTube channel, and I hope that one of them will bloody well see it and go wow that's just not on. A big issue you see is the nurses who go care for us; they haven't got a clue what's going on. In every other bit of medicine, the nurses would know what to do in aftercare, whereas you get these nurses walk in, they whip back the sheet and see this brand new willy, they haven't got a clue how it's supposed to go in a forty-five-degree angle and what padding to use, and all of that, and you can see they're scathing their heads off half the time, so they can't tell you what's going on, they don't know themselves. It's fragmented, it's very, very fragmented in the way it's done. But hey, it's the downside and a hell lot better than it was, and it will get better, that's also why I share, by sharing it then improves the next.

Tobias: *You said that you had reservations about sharing information on lower surgery, why is that?*

Finn: Well, it's a penis! [*laughs*] My chest is one thing, but actually getting your willy out for people to see is quite another. I was like, I'm really not sure if I want to do that—mainly because it's my genitals . . . but also I get the occasional bad comment on YouTube and I was really worried that I would get comments on my Tumblr, and you know, this is my new body part in progress—it's not finished, so I didn't want anyone to go "uh what's that!?" So that's what worried me about being out there, but in the end I just put a picture out there and if it went badly I would just take it away.

Tobias: *It's interesting that people happily document their top surgery in very intimate ways and yet, there is a boundary when it comes to phalloplasty, what are your thoughts on that?*

Finn: It's so sexualized. Chests aren't sexualized so much, but a penis is, and that's the thing, I think. For me, there is NO WAY that I would show it on YouTube . . . it does feel very different. Because a picture is kind of flat, lifeless—it's just an image, whereas a video of me with my willy in my hand, no no!

Tobias: *So there is a difference between a photo and a video—a photo is more decontextualized, cut off from your face and—*

Finn: Yeah, I can choose a photo when my willy looks the prettiest, you know, but you can't do that on YouTube. . . . It does feel very different, it's a static image and not my naked self as in a video.

Tobias: *Do you feel vulnerable in another way—exposing that body part?*

Finn: [*Nods eagerly*] It's vulnerability, but it's also boundaries. I feel very vulnerable all the time sharing on YouTube, the payoff is enough to outweigh it. I guess that I share so much of me that I don't want all of me everywhere, so I guess that's why I put things in bits, so that there is not all of me in one place, if that makes sense.

Tobias: *Now that you are having some corrections done, do you search on YouTube yourself?*

Finn: Yeah, yeah, because I've had this ureteral stricture so I've gone to search and see if other people have had that and how they got through it. Very much so—I still do that. I don't go for gender transition stuff, but when it comes to lower surgery stuff, yeah I do. Because in terms of complications London don't document at all, they tell us the stages, but they don't really talk about what can happen. I mean, I didn't know that they were gonna open me back up, I thought that I was gonna get a tiny hole, so they didn't even tell me that. So it's things like that, so the only way to get information about that is to talk to other guys who've had similar stuff happened and what they've done.

Tobias: *Do you have a specific audience in mind when you do the vlogs about lower surgery?*

Finn: Well, my Tumblr stuff is *just* for trans people, hopefully just for trans people that are looking for surgery, whereas YouTube is for anyone. In fact, I hope with YouTube to reach people who aren't trans in terms of information. . . . It's another reason why I don't share my stuff on YouTube because it would just be voyeurism and you get cis-gendered people just looking for trans willys and what not, whereas it's not so easy to find that on Tumblr, and people can't be bothered to read can they? Most trolls would go on YouTube because they can quickly find a video and make an awful comment about someone, so that's another reason why the two platforms work very differently, I think.

Tobias: *Tumblr seems to have some of the activist and anarchistic touch and feeling that YouTube had in the beginning. Do you feel that change within YouTube?*

Finn: Yeah, definitely. YouTube has become much more strict, cutting people off. There is a huge uproar actually because most of their restricted cuts are of LGBT content. So yeah, that's a big issue. Right, beforehand it was like you can put anything on YouTube and nobody would raise an eyelid whereas now it's very different.

Tobias: *YouTube also encourages a different kind of interaction now. You need to sell yourself.*[1] *What are your thoughts about that?*

Finn: I struggle with that. You know, I have refused to monetize my content for ages, I have only monetized in the last year and a half—I mean I don't—I only get ten pound a month or something like that. Answering comments is a good hour a day, so I thought, "fair enough if I get a little money back for doing it." But you see I would love to do this for a living—this is why I'm studying to be a psychologist—but what I really love is the kind of talking and interacting with people on YouTube, so I don't know if there is a way to actually turn that into a job at some point. I am now embracing the idea of selling myself a bit, which is also why I have started to develop other kinds of social medias . . . so there is the need to get my name known and things like that but yeah, it feels eekie in some ways. But I argue about this a lot. In our society we have this issue going on that by doing something good you are supposed to not get paid for it . . . and there is no reason to feel eekie for a lack of better word, but it does, it feels weird. So I try to not do too much of this "subscribe now!" It just doesn't feel real.

Tobias Raun, the New Media section editor, is an assistant professor of communication studies at the University of Roskilde (Denmark). He is the author of "DIY Therapy: Exploring Affective Self-Representations in Trans Video Blogs on YouTube" in *Digital Cultures and the Politics of Emotion* (2012).

Note

1.   YouTube has been heavily commercialized, and, especially within recent years, the site's distinction between amateur material/user generated content (UGC) and commercial material/professionally generated content (PGC) has become difficult to maintain. The culture of the so-called pro-ams has spread, and many producers of UGC now produce videos for YouTube as their main profession as a result of, for example, the YouTube Partner program, ad revenue, and sponsored content. Hence self-commodification is today an integrated part of self-presentation on YouTube, which is maybe most explicitly illustrated in the short "welcome to my channel video" that almost every YouTuber has today. The pressing question has become how to "promote oneself" or how to "grow one's channel," and YouTube itself offers extensive guidelines for just that. In sum, YouTube as a platform and the self-presentation of individual vloggers have undergone an increasing commercialization.

References

Cotton, Trystan T. 2012. *Hung Jury: Testimonies of Genital Surgery by Transsexual Men*. Oakland, CA: Transgress.

FinnTheInficible. 2017a. YouTube. www.youtube.com/user/FinnTheInfinncible.

———. 2017b. Tumblr. finntheinfinncible.tumblr.com.

———. 2017c. Facebook. www.facebook.com/finntheinfinncible/.

———. 2017d. Finlay Games. finlaygames.com.

Raun, Tobias. 2012. "DIY Therapy: Exploring Affective Self-Representations in Trans Video Blogs on YouTube." In *Digital Cultures and the Politics of Emotion: Feelings, Affect, and Technological Change*, edited by Athina Karatzogianni and Adi Kuntsman, 165–80. New York: Palgrave Macmillan.

———. 2015a. "Archiving the Wonders of Testosterone via YouTube." *TSQ* 2, no. 4: 701–9.

———. 2015b. "Video Blogging as a Vehicle of Transformation: Exploring the Intersection between Trans Identity and Information Technology." *International Journal of Cultural Studies* 18, no. 3: 365–78.

———. 2016a. *Out Online: Trans Self-Representation and Community Building on YouTube*. New York: Routledge.

———. 2016b. "The 'Caspian Case' and Its Aftermath: Transgender People's Use of Facebook to Engage Discriminatory Mainstream News Coverage in Denmark." In *New Dimensions of Diversity in Nordic Culture and Society*, edited by Jenny Björklund and Ursula Lindqvist, 77–99. Cambridge: Cambridge Scholars.

Raun, Tobias, and Cael Keegan. 2017. "Nothing to Hide: Selfies, Sex, and the Visibility Dilemma in Trans Male Online Cultures." In *Sex in the Digital Age*, edited by Paul G. Nixon and Isabel K. Dusterhoft, 89–100. New York: Routledge.

Coming to Terms with the Queer Past
A Critical Perspective on Magnus Hirschfeld's Legacy

JAVIER SAMPER VENDRELL

The Hirschfeld Archives: Violence, Death, and Modern Queer Culture
Heike Bauer
Philadelphia: Temple University Press, 2017. 230 pp.

On September 7, 2017, the Lesbian and Gay Federation of Berlin-Brandenburg (LSVD) unveiled a monument for the first homosexual emancipation movement. The memorial is composed of six thirteen-foot calla lilies in rainbow colors. The chosen flower, according to the organization, "has feminine and masculine blooms in one plant and is therefore a symbol for the normality of sexual and gender diversity in nature" (LSVD 2017). The monument was erected on the Magnus-Hirschfeld-Ufer, a promenade along Berlin's Spree River near the German chancellery. Its representation of the natural basis of gender and sexual diversity conveys the ideas of Dr. Magnus Hirschfeld, one of the founders of the world's first homosexual rights organization, the Scientific Humanitarian Committee, in 1897. The colorful monument, according to the organization's newsletter, has "a positive and confident effect" (LSVD 2017). These are important features for a memorial that seeks to counteract another one dedicated to homosexuals persecuted under Nazism, which is located not far away from it. The coexistence of these two monuments is representative of the difficulty of reconciling affirmative histories with those of violence and death that, according to Heike Bauer, underlie modern queer culture.

I begin the review of Heike Bauer's book *The Hirschfeld Archives: Violence, Death, and Modern Queer Culture* with this anecdote because it is significant for the uncritical and quasi-hagiographic treatment that Magnus Hirschfeld has received by historians in Germany and abroad. Hirschfeld is a staple of queer

TSQ: Transgender Studies Quarterly ∗ Volume 5, Number 2 ∗ May 2018
DOI 10.1215/23289252-4348734 © 2018 Duke University Press

histories that rely on "foundational moments" (133), such as Oscar Wilde's trial, the Stonewall riots, the AIDS crisis, and, in Germany, the founding of Hirschfeld's Institute for Sexual Science and its destruction by the Nazis in 1933. Why is Hirschfeld uncritically celebrated as a "founding father" of the LGBTQIA movement, when so many of his ideas seem dated or problematic? Why do we celebrate an early sexologist, despite the harm that science has done—and continues to do—to queer individuals? While this is not the place to answer these questions, Bauer's important book sheds critical insight into Hirschfeld and his role in the development of a homosexual rights movement in Germany.

Hirschfeld is undoubtedly an important historical figure for queer and trans studies. According to Susan Stryker, he "was a pivotal figure in the political history of sexuality and gender" and "a pioneering advocate for transgender people" (2008: 38–39). He introduced the concept "transvestite" in 1910 and documented trans lives throughout his life. Furthermore, Hirschfeld has received renewed attention in pop culture. Bauer begins the book with a discussion of the television show *Transparent*. The show's trans character Gittel, one of Maura Pfefferman's (Jeffrey Tambor) German-Jewish relatives, captures the imbricated histories of homophobia and transphobia, anti-Semitism, and the Holocaust. The re-created historical scenes in the show, which take place at Hirschfeld's institute, illustrate how "the lives of people whose bodies and desires do not conform to binary social norms and expectations have been subjected to violence across time" (2). Readers expecting a biography will be disappointed: they may be directed to the books by Ralf Dose (2014) and Manfred Herzer (2001). Instead, Bauer focuses on Hirschfeld's blind spots, namely, his condoning or downplaying colonialism, racism, gender violence, and child abuse, and his tendency to silence the voices he claimed to stand up for: queer people and women.

The Hirschfeld Archives is heir to the affective turn in queer theory and its focus on negative feelings, such as shame. The author draws heavily from the insights of Sara Ahmed, Heather Love, Ann Cvetkovich, and Carla Freccero to stress the need to move past histories of positive recovery and affirmation, which often focus on white gay men. Bauer argues that "the past is populated by those awkward queer subjects whose place in affirmative or redemptive histories is brought into question by cruelties they have committed, aligning themselves with oppressive politics or simply remaining silent on, and appearing unmoved by, the violence of injustices of their time" (8). This position requires a critical reassessment of Hirschfeld's work. Undoubtedly, racism and homophobia impacted Hirschfeld's life. Yet we risk an uncritical interpretation of history if we focus only on victimhood. His work for homosexual emancipation was not free from the violence that racism and sexism bring upon queer individuals. As Bauer's analysis of the sexologist's writings demonstrates, "emerging homosexual rights activism was itself imbricated in everyday racism and colonial violence" in the first three decades of the twentieth century (2). Throughout the book, Bauer conducts a careful disentangling of the different forms of oppression that come into view in Hirschfeld's writings. Nevertheless, the book should not be seen as a controversial onslaught on the respected sexologist but as a lesson about the implications of these forms of oppression in modern queer culture and activism. Evoking Walter Benjamin, Bauer refers to a painting by Paul Klee, *One Who Understands* (1934), the image on the book's cover, to problematize the idea of queer progress and to remind us that there is a "paradoxical disjuncture between the sociopolitical gains that have improved queer lives collectively and the experiences of violence" that queer people experience (9).

In the first chapter, Bauer takes apart Hirschfeld's little-known book *Racism*, some of his jingoistic pieces written on the eve of the First World War, and his support of eugenics and German colonialism to remind us that "emerging homosexual rights discourses cannot be separated from the racial injustice and colonial violence of the modern period" (35). Chapter 2 focuses on death and suicide, especially in the accounts of the patients whose experiences Hirschfeld recorded. Bauer argues that "queer suicide and violent deaths are part of a traumatic collective experience, markers of the potentially lethal force of heteronormative ideals and expectations but also complex sites of shared identification and resistance" (37). Hirschfeld acknowledged that "homosexual suicide" was not caused by some congenital defect but, rather, by the pressures of heteronormativity (47). Gender and sexual social norms drove queer individuals to depression, despair, and, ultimately, to their deaths. According to Bauer, these testimonies "show that homosexual culture formed not just around political protest and affirmative cultural representations but also around injury, hurt, and death" (56). Reading this chapter brought to mind the cases of Matthew Shepard and Brandon Teena. Their deaths are part of a collective queer and trans consciousness based on violence and trauma. Their stories, as Judith Halberstam argues, should be used "to create an archive capable of providing a record of the complex interactions of race, class, gender, and sexuality that result in murder, but whose origins lie in state-authorized formations of racism, homophobia, and poverty" (2005: 46). The attention their murders received in the media is symptomatic of the complexities Bauer wishes to stress: whiteness made them worthy of public attention. In contrast, the many trans women of color murdered regularly are overlooked in the media and do not become the impetus for legislative change. Activists such as Lourdes Ashley Hunter at the TransWomen of Color Collective raise awareness about such inconsistencies and contradictions in white queer activism.

In chapter 3 Bauer shifts the focus to abuse. Hirschfeld's writings, Bauer argues, are testimony to the normalization of intimate violence in early twentieth-century Germany. Attention to abuse and sexual violence in his work shows "that homosexuality, and the violence against it, did not emerge in isolation but in a space of habitual normal cruelty against bodies constructed as weak, perverse, or abhorrent" (58). Hirschfeld's interest in dissociating pedophilia from homosexuality, for example, something he deemed necessary to help decriminalize male same-sex acts, created a blind spot for child abuse; his reinforcement of binary gender, even though he generally argued that gender was undetermined, justified surgical intervention in intersex infants.

Bauer continues to focus on the links between different forms of oppression in the next chapter. Here, Bauer examines the blurry boundaries between the private and public lives of those living at Hirschfeld's institute. An insightful analysis of the educational displays that decorated the institute shows how that space fostered "queer kinship," even among those, like Christopher Isherwood, who felt unease at first. The public function of the institute was "transformative" for those who inhabited and walked through it (91). The destruction at the hands of the Nazis sought to halt that process. The Nazi attack, moreover, illustrates the "blurring of boundaries between antisemitism and homophobia" (100) that affected Hirschfeld and his collaborators.

Before the rise of the Nazis and the destruction of the institute, Hirschfeld had embarked on a world tour that turned into exile. He never returned to his native country. During his travels around the world, Hirschfeld met his younger partner, Tao Li, and a host of sexologists and feminist activists. Bauer shows, however, that this world tour also signaled Hirschfeld's public abandonment of what had been his mission in life: speaking up for the rights of queer individuals. In the United States, Japan, India, and Egypt, he focused instead on heterosexuality and marital love. This shift, Bauer suggests, "seems to have been a direct response to the perilousness of his political exile" and not the result of shame or secrecy (105). His world travels also signal a more important shift. An analysis of his book *Die Weltreise eines Sexualforschers* (1933), published in English in 1935 as *Men and Women: The World Journey of a Sexologist*, "is a reminder that prejudice can lurk in unacknowledged ways even in projects that overtly proclaim their own progressiveness and solidarity with oppressed people" (117). Despite Hirschfeld's credentials as a progressive doctor and feminist, he *speaks for* women in *The World Journey*. His travels in Palestine show another blind spot: his sympathy for the colonizers' manliness and vitality does not allow him to see the displacement and violence that any form of colonialism brings about. "Despite Hirschfeld's own life and death being subjected to violence because of his sexual reform work and Jewishness, his account of his travels shows that contrary to his political claims he did not always fully apprehend everyone on equal terms," Bauer states (124). It is fair to include Hirschfeld in a list of other European expert observers, such as Bronisław Malinowski, who had an ambivalent position to colonialism. Ultimately, Hirschfeld was a man of his time. Yet Bauer's goal is not to discredit him but to highlight that "affirmative global homosexual politics could retain and perpetuate practices that support discrimination and exclusion even when speaking out for justice" (124).

The book ends with a reflection on Hirschfeld's "afterlife" in the postwar years. Alfred Kinsey recognized him as an important pioneer in the field of sexology. However, Kinsey dismissed his work: "Hirschfeld's homosexuality disqualified him as a scientist" (128). Kinsey's dismissal indicates "the 'straight turn' of sex research" after the war (132), a turn that Hirschfeld arguably started himself. The links between homosexuality and communism under McCarthyism marked the postwar homophobic backlash in the United States. In Germany, the twisted link between National Socialism and homosexuality persisted after the war. Recovery from these forms of homophobic backlash should not prevent critical assessment of historical figures such as Hirschfeld and the oppression that underlies his work. Bauer's book pushes us to think about the centrality of feminism, antiracism, and anti-imperialism in queer politics and activism. It is a necessary read for anybody interested in queer social justice and history.

Javier Samper Vendrell is an assistant professor of German studies at Grinnell College. He is currently completing a book about the history of homosexuality, youth, and mass culture in the Weimar Republic. He can be reached at samperja@grinnell.edu.

References

Dose, Ralf. 2014. *Magnus Hirschfeld: The Origins of the Gay Liberation Movement*. New York: Monthly Review.

Halberstam, Judith. 2005. *In a Queer Time and Place: Transgender Bodies, Subcultural Lives*. New York: New York University Press.

Herzer, Manfred. 2001. *Magnus Hirschfeld: Leben und Werk eines jüdischen, schwulen und sozialistischen Sexologen* (*Magnus Hirschfeld: The Life and Work of a Jewish, Gay, and Socialist Sexologist*). Hamburg: MännerschwarmSkript.

LSVD (Lesbian and Gay Federation of Berlin-Brandenburg). 2017. "Denkmal für die erste Homosexuellenbewegung" ("Monument for the First Homosexual Movement"). *LSVD Newsletter*, September 1. www.sendcockpit.com/appl/ce/software/code/ext/_ns.php?&uid=eedf25c23039a2986b2d2bfd62434649.

Stryker, Susan. 2008. *Transgender History*. Berkeley, CA: Seal.

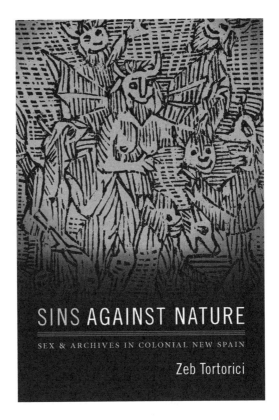

JOURNAL OF THE HISTORY OF SEXUALITY

Volume 26 Number 2

May 2017

UNIVERSITY OF TEXAS PRESS

Post Office Box 7819, Austin, Texas 78713-7819
P: 512.471.7233 | F: 512.232.7178 | journals@utpress.utexas.edu
UTPRESS.UTEXAS.EDU

Keep up to date on new scholarship

Issue alerts are a great way to stay current on all the cutting-edge scholarship from your favorite Duke University Press journals. This free service delivers tables of contents directly to your inbox, informing you of the latest groundbreaking work as soon as it is published.

To sign up for issue alerts:

1. Visit **dukeu.press/register** and register for an account. You do not need to provide a customer number.

2. After registering, visit **dukeu.press/alerts**.

3. Go to "Latest Issue Alerts" and click on "Add Alerts."

4. Select as many publications as you would like from the pop-up window and click "Add Alerts."

read.dukeupress.edu/journals